created to be *creative*

Arleen Jennings

TATE PUBLISHING *& Enterprises*

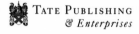
TATE PUBLISHING
& Enterprises

Book design copyright © 2006 by Tate Publishing, LLC. All rights reserved.
Cover design by Melanie Harr-Hughes
Interior design by Lauren Weatherholt

Published in the United States of America

ISBN: 1-5988644-1-6
06.09.14

To my husband Ron
You have made my life wonderful!

table of contents

acknowledgments

First, I want to thank my youngest daughter, Colleen: I appreciate your love for literature, the editing skills you've already developed, and your help typing major portions of my manuscript.

Brenda Rigby Riehle: Thanks for reading my first draft and encouraging me anyway. I also appreciate your willingness to read my final manuscript on short notice and give some valuable suggestions. You are a true friend.

Stephanie Dean: Without you, this book would have never made it to print. Beyond your editing skills, you picked up the heart of this project, and more importantly, you taught me to write better without losing personal expression. Thanks!

To my husband Ron: I am grateful for your labor of love in helping with final edits even though your plate was already extremely full. I appreciate your integrity and your many words of wisdom, which have positively strengthened this book. I love you!

Ted Murphy: Thank you for your support and for believing in this project. Your willingness to take time during the busy Spring Semester to write my foreword is greatly appreciated.

Janet Lang: Thanks for reading through the complete manuscript and finding those elusive typos.

Patty Stalker: Thanks for your help, advice, and support.

Suzanne Cadden: I enjoy seeing you grow as an artist. Thanks for sharing your painting used at the beginning of Section Three. I wish it could have been in color, it is amazing.

I also want to thank my daughter, Jessica: Your graphics help bring this book to life.

To my children, Karen, Stephen, Jessica, Brian, and Colleen: It is fun to watch your talents develop and to see how God is going to use them for His glory. I am so thankful for each one of you.

To my Pastor, Pat Lyons: It is a privilege to serve the Lord with you. I often find inspiration from your sermons and apply it to my art . . . as well as to my life. Thank you for your commitment to the Lord and your heart to lead.

Pam Russo: Thanks for photographing the artwork for this book.

My thanks and gratitude to all the great people at Tate Publishing. I would especially like to thank Janey Hays: Your enthusiasm over the contents of this book refreshed my passion and my purpose.

Finally, I would be remiss if I did not thank my Lord and Savior Jesus Christ. I am so thankful I know You personally and I appreciate the gifts and talents You have given me. Even though developing them hasn't come easy, You've challenged me to practice my own preaching and have brought me further than I ever thought possible. I am forever grateful and may You be glorified through these pages!

foreword

I was a junior in college when I was asked by Pastor Tom Nees of The Community of Hope in the inner city of Washington DC, to help deliver gifts to the families of the building where the church was housed. That was in the late 70's. The riots of racial anger and the upheaval from the Civil Rights Movement (via Martin Luther King's assassination) were still smoldering in the stretches of Belmont and Fourteen Street.

I agreed to help distribute baskets of fruit to the families, all of them in desperate poverty. As I walked from apartment to apartment to extend the gifts of the church, I was struck by one consistent fact. Despite how poor each family was, some decorative element was visible in every home. These were not works of art, these were not things of value, but they held significant meaning.

Walker Evans and James Agee made the same observation regarding the impulse to decorate among the southern poor in the 1930's. Evans' photographs reveal a world of poverty that shocked Americans everywhere. But look closely at those photographs published in *Let Us Now Praise Famous Men*. The walls are covered with the "funny papers." Cartoons from the newspaper functioned as wallpaper for people who could never afford real wallpaper. This was *all* they had to transform their environment. It served as a "kind" of creative reaction to their poverty.

It is a mistake among many that art is peripheral, something that only comes after the serious things in life have been addressed. Too often this is the message in our public schools. When cuts are made, they are first made to music and art programs. If questioned, the Board Members have a look of shock; their faces say, "But math, science, and writing, these are the core of education . . ."

I have taught at both the high school and college level. I can say with great confidence that art and, by extension, music, are not "extras" to the development of young students. They are essential.

Arleen Jennings' book *Created to be Creative* takes seriously the attribute of the creativity of God and illustrates how this characteristic in people is a reflection of God's creative nature. It is not a choice we have but a mandate. We are called to perform creative acts because we are made in God's image.

Art is about communication. Communication through a very specific language of images, sounds, poetic words, and dance are forms. Communication is essential to our humanness. Only the dullest of thinkers believe that ordinary language is sufficient to address all the experiences of life.

The communication that the arts add to the way in which people express aspects of the heart is critical. It is also a continuum. Art does not progress in the way that technology progresses. It is for this reason we value so much the artistic achievements of the past. As Ben Johnson said of Shakespeare, "He was not for an age but for all time." The ideas revealed in Titian's *Man with a Glove* do not diminish through time. The mysteries live on in this painting as the meanings in the words of Proust, Keats, or Borges.

Arleen's plea is that great art is not the only art worth making, she advocates that the creative act itself is vital and life enriching. It is also an act of worship. By this she rightly asserts that choosing to develop the creativity within us helps to *undermine those things which seek to undermine us as persons created by a creative God.*

The focus is not upon the object but the object-making. Quality has its place. As a professor of Art, I am required to instill in my students a sense of quality. But quality is a moving target. It takes exposure to many fine examples of the craft to develop this important sense of quality. However, the courage to create should not be undermined by this pursuit of quality. The very act of making something has its own rewards. I have seen on many occasions how the arts have salvaged students on the brink of despair. Journaling, acting, music, visual arts—these activities nourish emotional needs.

Our culture has wrongly assumed that criticism of a person's creative attempts will frustrate and derail their future confidence. If all criticism is negative, this could become true. However, any observation of the passion in young people for athletics challenges this assumption. Coaches have high expectations and offer frequent criticism aimed at inspiring performance. I see no decline in sports in this country. On the contrary, it has reached in some communities a near hysterical pitch.

Arleen's call is one for balance, for keeping both views in focus. She is keenly aware that art-making and creative expression can and will have failure. But we should not be cowards who have been called by God to exercise our gifts. For this reason, Arleen points to the importance of community. It is not that we individually strive to make works of great significance, but that we participate in the grand tradition of the creative process.

The recent research in multiple intelligences clearly establishes that people are smart in ways previously described as "talented." Tradition says that mathematicians are smart, artists are talented. Today it is more correctly understood that art making or music making is also a kind of intelligence. This being the case, people should take stock in the realization that what they are excellent at differs merely in kind but not degree to other more traditional measures of intellect.

Those seeking encouragement to shake off their inhibitions and plunge into this creative process will find much in this text to prod them forward.

The creative act is an expression of love in the same way in which children are the physical manifestation of love in a marriage. Love is always "green" according to E.E. Cummings. Green because it is alive.

Theodore J. Murphy, MFA,
Professor of Art, Houghton College

introduction

Dear Reader,

It is important for you to understand that you're not alone in your quest to unleash and use the creative side of you. Therefore, I have written this book in the "we" and "us" format as much as possible. The examples given show why many people feel isolated and afraid to try creative ventures. This book addresses many internal, as well as external, issues that hinder us and is as much about life as it is about finding and using our talents. It also shows us how and where to begin the journey so that we can find greater purpose in and through the things we do.

When I use the word *art,* I'm including all creative activity. Though this book favors the traditional arts, it is not meant to be exclusive; simply insert your form of *creative outlet* (a term used often) into the examples given. Then apply these principles to your individual situation. No matter what your outlets are—cooking, scrapbooking, interior decorating, landscaping, gardening, woodworking, photography, etc., the concepts set forth in this book will apply to you.

☞ *If you already have a creative outlet, this book will encourage you to look deeper than the surface, think past the obvious, and learn how to make your form of art speak.*

☞ *If you know you have talent, but aren't sure what to do with it or how to find a creative outlet, and you want direction toward increasing your ability, keep reading.*

☞ *If you feel you don't have any natural ability, put that thought aside as you flip through these pages. Then open your eyes, your ears, and most importantly your heart, so you can learn to recognize your talents and experience creative fulfillment. By the way, don't get discouraged if it takes some time to discover what's right for you; this is simply part of the process.*

I divided this book into four sections. The first section focuses on who we are in Christ and accepting the fact that we were born with a creative nature. It also gives constructive ideas of how to successfully find and faithfully use creative outlets. If you are already an experienced artist, you may be tempted to dismiss the first section, but please read it anyway. I am confident there are concepts that will help you. It will also make you aware of some of the insecurities that people face and why they're afraid to try creative things. As you read, think of ways that you can encourage others to take up a creative outlet. You will be doing them a favor.

Section two speaks about our need for effort and making art a priority. Additional elements are also crucial in reaching our full potential: the need to *slow down* and improve our observation skills, learn how to think more creatively about everything, and the importance of taking creative action.

The third section gets into the meat of this book. It is of utmost importance that we realize there are godly boundaries when it comes to our creative outlets. It is time for Christians to become more involved in the arts so we can have a greater influence on society.

The fourth and last section deals with the hindrances that try to keep us from creative living. We will learn why these distractions are detrimental to our health and our purpose. Creative outlets are good for us and can help us through tough times; these chapters will show us how.

Above all, this book will help us discover how we can employ our talents in God's service and increase our opportunities to witness. If this concept is new to you, don't feel pressured into thinking you have to go public with your creative outlet right away, there is usually a grace period for personal growth. Some of you may never *go public* with your talents, but don't be surprised when you find creative expression brings encouragement and refreshing on a personal level. This will in turn strengthen you to labor for God in other ways by using your individual personality to minister to those He brings across your path. And who knows, once you're comfortable with the development of your abilities, you may find God wants you to share your talents with others. As you begin to understand the full scope of the creative experience and its benefits, I pray Jesus will show you the direction He would have you take.

Ecclesiastes 7:8 tells us, "The end of a thing is better than its beginning . . ." but you cannot get to the end without a beginning! Creativity has to start somewhere. Some of you have pursued artistic endeavors from your youth and already understand the benefits of having a creative outlet. A number of you did creative things while in school, but then never kept at them, and you're feeling the urge to pick them up again. Maybe you have only recently started a creative outlet. This book will show you the importance of sticking with it and what can be gained by doing so. Then there are those of you who are about to discover your creative side, that is why you're reading this book. It doesn't matter where you are at this point, because we can all grow in the area of talents and discover the many wonderful ways creative action can improve our lives. From here, God can reveal His plan for using our abilities for *His good pleasure* and show us how our gifts can add meaning to the lives of others by their interaction with our creative expression.

So, whether you've already begun, or if today is the day of your beginning, please determine in your heart to continue, even when it's not easy or when distractions come. Be assured, how much of a difference this book makes in your life will be determined by how much you are willing to apply these concepts and take creative action. Thinking about them is not enough. I am amazed by how much the writing of this book has changed my life for good. I've had opportunity to practice these principles and I know first hand they work. As you read, open your heart to the creative possibilities that are within your grasp and use your talents as only you can.

Arleen Jennings

section one

conquer insecurities, discover talents

dare to be real

chapter one

born with a creative nature

In the beginning God created the heavens
and the earth. Genesis 1:1

All creativity begins with God, but it does not end there. Genesis 1:27 tells us we are created in the image of God. Through this divine connection, creative potential passed from heaven to earth, from God to man. By doing so, our Creator established a way to interact with humanity, making us partakers of His nature.

This creative urge is stronger and more defined in some and they often want to share their talents with the world. However, many of us don't know what talents we possess or how to discover them, leaving us to wonder if the innovative resources within us can be aroused. Be assured they most certainly can.

Compare the prospect of success in any creative endeavor to the aspirations and ability of athletes. Just because someone is not a phenomenal athlete doesn't mean the door is closed to participating in a sport for fun. We can find pleasure and physical benefits from taking part in such activities, even if we don't have an abundance of *natural talent*. Moreover, keeping things in perspective, one who is proficient at tennis may not excel in distance running. When it comes to sports, we find what interests us and then work at exercising and developing those skills. The same should be true with creativity. For example, if I asked how many of you can sing well, a number of you would respond favorably and acknowledge your ability. Then if I changed my question to how many of you simply enjoy singing, most, if not all, would admit you *like to* sing: in the shower, along with the radio, at church . . . demonstrating that you don't have to be an exceptional vocalist to enjoy singing, and so forth.

Giving our creative side an opportunity to show its worth is something that can and should be done, even if at first, we feel like we are on the low end of the talent scale. We could liken it to having *patience*. Long-suffering is indicative of God's nature and a fruit of the Spirit; therefore, it should be exhibited in our lives. Now, some have more patience than others, but this does not excuse any of us from maturing in the area of self-control. All growth makes us better for God's service, including the development of talents.

Recognizing our individual levels of creative desire must be the first step, because here the journey begins. Some have clear-cut ambition toward a specific form of art; they know what they like and what they want to accomplish, boldly moving toward their goals without reservation. Others have ambition but seem threatened by the fear of failure or the opinions of others. Then there are those who just need some free time or motivation to find a creative outlet. It is often easy, especially in our culture, to find ourselves too busy to bother with creative pursuits. Finally, there will be a few who say they have no desire to be creative. However, that does not negate the fact that we are all born with a creative nature; and talents are easier to discover than you may realize. Besides, creativity goes further than the *traditional arts,* so open your heart to the possibilities.

Taking creative action is about more than the ability to draw or paint, sing or play an instrument; it shows up in everything we do. Though we build homes, work, raise families, cook, and do all the necessary things to survive, we are not content with this. We crave diversity and must create. Our homes have unique character and possess interest far beyond a roof over our heads. Most houses differ one from another and the personality of the owner is reflected in the appearance of each, inside and out. Even in housing developments where all the structural framing of each house is the same, or in apartments where there may be no opportunity to revise the external structure, our homes are still distinctively furnished and individually adorned. We make choices by what appeals to us and then decorate accordingly; even those of us who hire professionals have a say in coordinating the interior design of our homes.

For those of you who don't think you're very creative, stop and take a good look around. Your creative nature is evident in your surroundings; from the colors you choose, to the style you like, to the ambiance you set. It's apparent at your work place, too: your organizational skills, your innovative ideas, and the way you express yourself. Creativity shows up in every aspect of daily life: how we think, the activities we enjoy, and the way we approach each situation. It affects how we dress and the way we do our hair. There's even diversity in our methods of preparing and serving food, making mealtime inviting as well as fulfilling.

Taking part in creative activities shouldn't seem intimidating or unattainable, because we naturally do it already. As you continue to read, you will find that creative possibilities are vast enough to include everyone and that God's purpose for the arts goes beyond personal pleasure, even though that is an important part of the process.

God's Creative Actions

Let's lay a foundation by looking at God's creative actions. They are more than a display of His awesome power and ability—they express His personality and the traits He passed on to us. For instance,

He uses size to reveal His infinite magnitude, placing us in a universe so vast that we cannot find its end. Yet, at the same time, He manifested His presence in the microscopic characteristics of an atom, whereby He holds all things together. The first proves His grandeur while the second demonstrates His concern and involvement with the smallest of all details, including our lives. "And He is before all things, and in Him all things consist" (Colossians 1:17).

God has a marvelous imagination. His handiwork contains exuberance and splendor at every turn. Some of His creative works are clearly seen in the artistic collection of beauty all around us, while others remain hidden. Romans 11:33 tells us, "Oh, the depth of the riches both of the wisdom and knowledge of God! How unsearchable are His judgments and His ways past finding out!" The more we learn about our world, the more we can learn about our Creator and His nature. "It is the glory of God to conceal a matter, but the glory of kings is to search out a matter" (Proverbs 25:2).

One significant reason for God making us in His likeness was for fellowship. Notice how Adam and Eve "heard the sound of the LORD God walking in the garden in the cool of the day" (Genesis 3:8). He never intended to be an abstract God, out of reach, and ready to chastise us if we don't comply with His every wish. Unfortunately, this is the perception many have of God, not understanding His heart or His desire to be intimately involved in our lives.

God is personable, and can "sympathize with our weaknesses . . ." (Hebrews 4:15). We can also learn a great deal about our Creator by studying the life of Jesus. "Who being the brightness of His glory and the express image of His person, and upholding all things by the word of His power, when He had by Himself purged our sins, sat down at the right hand of the Majesty on high" (Hebrews 1:3). Jesus came in the flesh, not only to save us, but also to give us a comprehendible look at God.

The more we understand His word, the more He reveals His

purpose for making us in His image. "For it is God who works in you both to will and to do for His good pleasure" (Philippians 2:13).

A Divine Plan

God's objectives involve more than imparting freedom to observe, think, and take creative action. It's about accepting who we are and using our talents as only we can. To help us understand His divine plan, let's look at the first day of Creation.

The destiny of an entire universe hung upon the thought process of Almighty God. First, He saw "the end from the beginning" (Isaiah 46:10). With the end determined, the plot began to take shape—God, in His timeless existence, with no beginning and no end, devised the creation of time and seasons, days and nights. The plan expanded and grew; humanity would be lost, kingdoms would rise and fall and a Savior would of necessity come. "Who has saved us and called us with a holy calling, not according to our works, but according to His own purpose and grace which was given to us in Christ Jesus before time began" (2 Timothy 1:9).

He then turned His focus on the beginning. Soon He would speak and day one would come into existence; but what would He create first? Why would His story require such a brilliant opening? A good author knows how to set the stage immediately, sparking the readers' interest and drawing them into the plot; not revealing too much, yet telling enough to captivate their thoughts, compelling them to find out what happens next. God, the *author* of creation and all living things had the beginning of His story now ready. The angels looked over the balcony of heaven to behold with wonder as God spoke, "Let there be light" (Genesis 1:3). LIGHT. The very first thing God created was light. Let's think about this for a moment—this light was not the sun, moon, nor stars; no, they were not created until the fourth day. So what was this light? What did it look like? It looked like GOD! The very first thing we know about the history of our world is that God created an expression of Himself. "God is light and in Him is no darkness at all" (1 John 1:5). His creation was to be filled with

His glory. The same glory spoken about in Isaiah 60:19, "The sun shall no longer be your light by day, nor for brightness shall the moon give light to you; but the LORD will be to you an everlasting light, and your God your glory." By the sixth day when man was created, he was not only able to see his surroundings because of light, but he could *see* light. Psalm 36:9 tells us, "For with You is the fountain of life; in Your light we see light." God made light so we could see Him everywhere we look and in everything we do.

Since God always leads by example, the creation of light set forth a divine principle: we have permission to create an expression of ourselves. God has empowered us to bring forth from within an outward display of the unique characteristics He has given us. One of the clearest ways to exhibit our individuality is through the arts. The medium, style, or kind of art we choose matters not—the size, shape, color, sound, or substance of what we produce is only a means to an end—as long as it illustrates who we are within the margins of God's word. In Chapter Ten, I will expand the concept of Godly Boundaries within the arts and the importance of keeping ourselves pure so that we can use our creative outlets as tools to witness. But first, we must learn how to creatively express His investment within us and be confident in our abilities so that we have something to share.

Because we live in a world that has fallen from its original created state, many of us feel trapped by the need to be, act like, or construct what we imagine others (not God) want. We worry about what people think of us and act accordingly; often missing God's purpose by trying to create or reproduce an ideal, rather than follow the heartbeat of truth. Individuality is the trademark of God's expression here on earth. Not only do no two people look exactly alike, none have the exact same personality. We ought to be thankful God made us unique, counting it a privilege.

Why then, do we try so hard to conform and feel like we won't fit in if we simply be whom God made us to be? In a lot of ways, being ourselves has become a lost form of art. Many have plunged into a state of confusion by desperately trying to become something they're not. God fashioned each of us according to the diversity of His own image. Therefore, it's wrong to clone our creativity or even our personality, in the image of limited human standards and expectations, especially when they are forever changing.

I ask you to search your heart; have you pursued an image you thought might make you rich or popular? Have you compromised your matchless expression to fit into what you thought was expected of you by others? Each of us has the opportunity to exhibit our worth like no one else and it is God's divine will that we do so.

First Things First

First and foremost, our identity has to be in Christ Jesus. If we do not know Him personally, nor respect His sovereignty, we cannot rightly represent His image. (The plan of salvation is explained in the *Appendix* for those who are not familiar with this terminology and would like to have a clearer understanding of its importance.)

Galatians 2:20 tells us how to accomplish this, "I am crucified with Christ: nevertheless I live; yet not I, but Christ liveth in me: and the life which I now live in the flesh I live by the faith of the Son of God, who loved me, and gave himself for me" (KJV). Notice the line, "Nevertheless I live." God does not kill our individuality, but He does want us to crucify the desires of our flesh. "For all that is in the world—the lust of the flesh, the lust of the eyes, and the pride of life—is not of the Father but is of the world" (1 John 2:16). These things do not characterize God's image. Each of us has a specific creative nature. However, because of the *fall of man,* we were all born in sin. "Likewise you also, reckon yourselves to be dead indeed to sin, but alive to God in Christ Jesus our Lord" (Romans 6:11). Sin and self-will must be crucified—but not individuality.

Devin has been a pastor for several years now, but this was not always the case. When he preached at our church, he shared a little of his testimony. Twenty plus years ago he wanted to be a rock star. He looked and acted the part; he even belonged to a band that traveled some distances to perform at bars and nightclubs. In the meantime, his wife Katrina had given her heart to Jesus, was going to church and didn't travel or sing with Devin any more. She did, however, faithfully pray for her husband's salvation. Things did not change immediately though, and after some length of time, Katrina was ready to give up on their marriage. The very evening she made plans to leave her husband, Devin was singing at a nightclub. As he looked out over the crowd of people, God opened his eyes to the realization they were lost in sin and so was he. That night he called Katrina and said he was coming home. He quit the band and gave his life to Jesus. Not long afterward, Devin and Katrina began to share the gospel through song, using their musical talents for God's service.

God gave Devin a great voice and musical ability, but before his conversion, he used his talents to promote sin and death. Today, Devin sings for Jesus. He doesn't look the same, he doesn't talk the same, and yet he lives—for Jesus. His personality was redeemed, not eliminated. Now his talents minister life and draw people to the saving grace of Jesus Christ.

Prototypes from the Bible

Let's look at a few examples of people God used in the Bible to see how their personalities promoted His purpose. Paul, (Saul, before his conversion,) had great zeal for the things of God, but not according to knowledge. He persecuted the church, imprisoning and killing many. When Paul met Jesus, his passionate personality remained intact, but the manner of his expression changed. He became zealous and useful to God, no longer destroying the church, but building it . . . God's way.

Then there's Peter, who was bold and often outspoken; even declaring, "Even if I have to die with You, I will not deny You" (Matthew 26:35)! We know Peter did deny Jesus; but he later repented and came to the place where he was "crucified with Christ." God didn't eradicate Peter's boldness, but He did adjust it, making this characteristic suitable for service. It was Peter who boldly stood up on the day of Pentecost and preached the first salvation message.

John was known as the "disciple whom Jesus loved." Do you know what John wrote the most about, especially in his first epistle? "Beloved, let us love one another" (1 John 4:7). There was a time though, when he was ready and willing, along with his brother James, to call fire down from heaven and destroy the people who rejected Jesus (Luke 9:54). John's love for the Lord caused him to be protective. He didn't understand that hurting others would not advance the Gospel. John's second and third epistles talk about walking in "truth and love." When I picture John, I see a person who had great passion for what is right, a no-compromise kind of man. Nevertheless, he had to learn that truth without love does not represent the heart of God. Again, the Lord made a necessary adjustment, but John's personality is still evident in the things he wrote and by the way he lived.

Did you know Luke's Gospel records the most healings of Jesus? It makes perfect sense; Luke was a physician, he liked helping people, and was interested in healing. God used his personality and skills in writing this portion of the Bible.

Can you see the correlation in all these situations? The character traits of each person were instrumental in the advancement of the Gospel. They are recorded in the Bible; not only for our example, but also for us to see the refined individuality of the people God called and used. It is His desire to use us as well.

Representing Jesus

Galatians 2:20 goes on to say, "Yet not I, but Christ liveth in me: and the life which I now live in the flesh I live by the faith of the Son of God, who loved me, and gave himself for me." When Jesus saves us, a transformation begins to take place from the unregenerate person we were, to the redeemed person we are becoming. And though God calls us to be individual and unique; it's of utmost consequence that our actions line up with His word.

> *That you put off, concerning your former conduct, the old man*
> *which grows corrupt according to the deceitful lusts, and be*
> *renewed in the spirit of your mind, and that you put on the*
> *new man which was created according to God, in true*
> *righteousness and holiness. (Ephesians 4:22–24)*

Our lives should be so full of Jesus that our actions represent Him well. He will require us to change our ways, when those ways don't reflect His image; but He has not called us to be robots either. It's okay to be creative in representing Jesus. You see, no one is exactly like me—only I can express that part of God's image. The same is true for you. Because of this, we should rejoice in how He made us and not try to be something or someone we're not. In order for God to accomplish His will in our lives, we must be mindful that it is not about us, but about "Christ in us, the hope of glory" (Colossians 1:27).

Remember, God knows the end from the beginning and has a plan to reach this lost and dying world. He does not speak from heaven (at least not very often) to save people, He has chosen to speak through us and commanded, "Go into all the world and preach the gospel to every creature" (Mark 16:15). Proverbs 3:6 instructs, "In all your ways acknowledge him, and he shall direct your paths." When we allow God's direction to flow through our creative outlets, He can use our unique expression to speak to those around us. This concept will be discussed further in Chapters Eleven and Twelve; however, some groundwork needs to be laid to prepare the way for our creative journey.

No Compromise

God, our perfect example, isn't worried about what people think of Him. He is not going to compromise the integrity of His nature or His will for a *better approval rating*. Colossians 1:16 states, "For by Him all things were created that are in heaven and that are on earth, visible and invisible, whether thrones or dominions or principalities or powers. All things were created through Him and for Him."

God creates with confidence and purpose. If you are insecure or feel trapped, stuck in performing for others more than being yourself, I pray the next chapter will help you find the strength you need to let your personality and creativity show forth the image of God . . . *let there be light*, let your God given ability to be creative shine.

chapter two

free from hidden identities

*Know that the LORD, He is God; it is He who has
made us, and not we ourselves; we are His people
and the sheep of His pasture. Psalm 100:3*

Legitimate success in creative endeavors is built upon our ability to be free from hidden identities. Many people worry about the impression they leave on others, fearful they won't be respected or able to live up to expectations, some even admitting they're *afraid to be real.*

Hiding is nothing new to the human race; it began in the Garden of Eden. Once Adam and Eve ate from the Tree of the Knowledge of Good and Evil, their eyes were opened and they knew they were naked. Shocked by the result of their rash decision, they panicked. What should they do? Their first inclination was to hide—but to hide from whom? They were the only two people. Ironically, they thought it necessary to hide from God. Frightened, they frantically searched the garden for a covering; finding fig leaves, they quickly gathered a bunch, sewed them together, and put them on. They must have thought God wouldn't notice . . . Nevertheless, as the story goes, they could not conceal their location or their shame. Their Creator knew right where they were and what they had done.

Genesis 3 frames the first great "cover up" of mankind. Hiding didn't work then and it doesn't work now. Jeremiah 23:24 tells us, "'Can anyone hide himself in secret places, so I shall not see him?' says the LORD. 'Do I not fill heaven and earth?' says the LORD." Simply stated, we cannot hide from God. However, we do think we can hide from people and as a result we wear the masks society expects from us; like the macho image "Men are not supposed to cry . . ." no matter what they are going through. "Women must have careers to be considered successful . . ." even if they are content to stay home and raise their children. Then there are those who work a job solely for monetary gain or prestige, though stress consumes their every waking moment. Trying to keep up with changing fashions is another disguise. If we were completely honest with ourselves, some of the styles we sport simply don't suit our personalities or help our image. These are just a few of the things we do to impress those around us, yet seldom do we consider the cost.

By embracing popular or accepted behaviors, we forego our God-given right to be unique and we lose sight of things that have lasting value. Our society is fickle—images, fashions, trends, and fame are ever changing. So why do we place our trust, or validate our worth, by the instability of such things, especially when God promises security? "For I am the LORD, I do not change" (Malachi 3:6).

The serpent tricked Eve into thinking she was not *good enough* the way God made her. Giving into this lie, she ate the forbidden fruit, but her action did not make her *wiser* or a *better person*. On the contrary, it activated the process of sickness, pain, toil, heartache, and death. The real problem arises from not being pleased with God's design, causing us to conform our image to worldly standards and empty promises. If we succumb to Eve's temptation of personal gain and earthly approbation, it weakens our witness and puts restraints on our ability to represent the image of God. We must be genuine with people if we want to show them the love of Jesus.

Unfortunately, some Christians even feel pressured to sport a mask at church, not willing or able to admit they need help with any of life's issues. Many feel they must demonstrate total control of every emotion, even if disaster strikes. Yet God took the time to record the flaws and passions of His people in the Bible so we could relate to His Word and the people He chose to use. It lifts the burden of thinking or feeling like we could never measure up.

I'm not talking about putting every feeling on public display. We need to control our emotions and learn to work through difficulties; but to hide our true temperament behind what is not real can be detrimental to the artistic nature within us. Authentic creative expression is impossible without coming to terms with who we really are and accepting the fact that we may feel vulnerable at times. While pretending, we imprison ourselves and the Spirit of God has no liberty to intervene; good emotions intertwine with the bad, and creativity is stifled along with our health and emotional well-being. Believing God created us with unique character traits and changeable emotions is invaluable because this enables us to use our God-given talents to their fullest potential.

Keep in mind, everyone experiences insecurities. The very ones we are looking to for affirmation may have their own desire for approval or acceptance and they are responding to us out of a personal need rather than noticing ours. Besides, people can be very inconsistent, sometimes acknowledging our efforts, while on other occasions overlooking them. I'm sure we've all done this at times, yet it's not fair to put such pressures on each other by trying to figure out every response to every action. This needlessly causes confusion, whereby making us susceptible to rejection instead of confident in God.

Accepting Diversity

One day, while having a heart to heart conversation with my

daughter, Colleen, concerning an incident that occurred among her friends, she pointed out, "Not only do we try to be someone everybody likes, but we can be guilty of trying to *be* someone else, other than who God made us to be." 1 Corinthians 12:15–18 puts it this way,

> *If the foot should say, 'Because I am not a hand, I am not of the body,' is it therefore not of the body? And if the ear should say, 'Because I am not an eye, I am not of the body,' is it therefore not of the body? If the whole body were an eye, where would be the hearing? If the whole were hearing, where would be the smelling? But now God has set the members, each one of them, in the body just as He pleased.*

This verse makes me think of an orchestra. The conductor needs *all* the different instruments to achieve the full sound of a symphony. To illustrate, if the tuba were trying to play the part of the cello, not only would it sound discordant, the orchestra would lack the sound of the tuba and not be complete.

Together, we are God's symphony. He orders our steps, yet allows for a wide range of sounds and emotions. He enjoys our unique expressions and even permits conflict from time to time. God has written a great narrative about each one of us. We shouldn't be afraid to let the story unfold—uninhibited—ready to meet the challenges of life head on. We must also realize our individual personalities and talents came with a specific destiny that we alone can fulfill. God has equipped each of us for success.

Hid With Christ

To hide behind the facade of worldly standards just to be accepted or to receive the praise of men is wrong. "Let me not, I pray, show partiality to anyone; nor let me flatter any man" (Job 32:21). Yet Psalm 17:8 tells us where we can hide: "Keep me as the apple of Your eye; hide me under the shadow of Your wings." Colossians 3:3 adds, " . . . and your life is hidden with Christ in God." As discussed in Chapter

One, this does not do away with our individuality. Instead, it enhances our capacity to be all that God created us to be. By allowing the Holy Spirit to intervene, we can properly deal with the negative emotions that come our way and be less apt to stay depressed or discouraged.

When it comes to discovering self-worth, our perspective must come from God's word. "Being confident of this very thing, that He who has begun a good work in you will complete it until the day of Jesus Christ" (Philippians 1:6). God already knows what we're going through, how we feel, our emotional condition, and even our weaknesses. Consequently, we needn't try to hide it from Him. We have the privilege of drawing close, allowing Him to nurture and strengthen us as we spend time in His presence. "I can do all things through Christ who strengthens me" (Philippians 4:13). It's not about being our own person outside of Jesus, but about putting " . . . on the new man who is renewed in knowledge according to the image of Him who created him" (Colossians 3:10).

Our creative nature will change and mature along with our personalities as we become more like Jesus. He is the one who empowers our confidence, directs our paths, gives us talents, and uses our lights to express Himself to the world. Once secure in Christ, our creative actions have the liberty to grow into a fulfilling facet of life.

How then do we free ourselves from the masks that conceal our God-given identities? Can we actually come to the place where life isn't a social masquerade? Yes, but this freedom can only come when we accept ourselves for whom we are and arrive at the place where we are content with the abilities God has given us. "Stand fast therefore in the liberty by which Christ has made us free, and do not be entangled again with a yoke of bondage" (Galatians 5:1).

Personal Expectations

Have you ever set goals that were impossible to achieve? Maybe your time frame wasn't realistic or your skills didn't match your expectations. If so, what happened? Unless you were very determined or willing to come up short and try again, you probably didn't meet your objective. The greater our resolve, the better chance we have in reaching our goals. Artistic ability, however, doesn't necessarily develop at the speed we predetermine, causing discouragement and possible defeat. We must be willing to learn and grow with the *process*, which will be discussed further in the next chapter.

Follow along as I lay some groundwork for finding creative fulfillment. Begin by putting the expectations of others out of mind, because the need to impress is like a rocky shoreline, ready at any moment to shipwreck your creative voyage. Next, put your artistic potential into proper perspective by taking inventory of your experience in the area of interest. Ask questions like: What do I want to accomplish? Why do I have such aspirations? How soon must my goals be achieved? Our answers frame our creative future and set us on the path of possibilities.

First, we should do it for ourselves. This eliminates external demands because there's no obligation to impress anyone or live up to someone else's expectations. We don't have to share results with others until we are ready, that way our creative outlets have a fair chance to flourish. When we feel in control of the things that try to intimidate us, our creative efforts have the opportunity to live, breathe, and become gratifying.

If down the road, our form of art blesses others, that's wonderful and will eventually become a part of our goal, but initially it can't be the consuming factor. Later in this book, I'll show the importance of using our talents for God. However, if we never attain the necessary skills because of outside influences—pressures to perform, fear of failure, or unrealistic personal goals—we won't have creative outlets that God can use. All these things are associated with hidden identities.

When I was in eighth grade, everyone in my class filled out a booklet which contained one hundred questions that had to do with our likes and dislikes. Its purpose was to help each of us decide on possible career opportunities and the classes we would need to take. We were to mark each question on a scale of one to four according to our interests. Thinking back to this assignment, all my choices had something to do with *art* and *writing*; but I never took writing seriously because I didn't like to read and my grades in English were very poor. It simply didn't seem feasible at the time to believe I could ever become an author. Regrettably, I put no effort toward this innate desire and allowed it to lay dormant for decades.

When the idea for this book first came to me, I felt intimidated because I had never written before. For me to be successful was going to take more than overcoming insecurities; I had to learn how to write. I needed to set goals and yet be reasonable as to how long it would take to reach them. I would also have to practice my own preaching by learning from the concepts put forth in these pages. To be sure, it didn't happen as quickly, or as smoothly, as I would have liked; but it was well worth my time and effort, both in creative fulfillment and in how it changed me as a person. Now you hold in your hands a testimony of my personal triumph in the ups and downs of developing a creative outlet.

One of the things that pushed me past my own fears and limitations was realizing that I wasn't the only one with unfulfilled dreams. Dealing with time shortages, performance issues, and a general fear of failure have kept many from enjoying artistic endeavors and, thus, reaping from their benefits.

I found purpose and personal gratification by taking time to develop and use the talents God has given me. The bars that once held my heart captive by the need for approval and the mask that concealed my insecurities are no longer relevant to who I am. Creativity has brought tremendous freedom to my life and my light shines brighter for Jesus because I've learned to *be*, and *like*, whom God has created me to be. The mask is gone. If you have experienced any of these anxieties, I pray you find the confidence and liberty you need to express yourself through the arts.

Lessons in the Sand

If you have ever been to the beach, you've probably seen a diverse range of sand sculptures: castles, sea urchins, animals, fish, and many other interesting things. A few will be masterfully done, others considered decent and some won't be much to look at. I have found the outcome doesn't really matter because none can withstand the crushing tide; yet the next day people return to build other "art forms" that will inevitably be expunged again. Why do they do this? For one, it's fun, and secondly, there's no pressure to succeed. It's simply an opportunity to be creative without worrying whether or not it's *good enough* because it won't stand long enough to make a difference. My children like to build sand walls around their castles to see which one will stand the longest, but in the end, all sculptures perish; even the biggest wall of sand cannot hold back the tide.

As the waves crash in and wash the sand smooth, it becomes an irresistible medium for creativity. Some find a freedom with sand that they cannot find on canvas or paper; these surfaces seem more intimidating because they carry with them a sense of permanence. Whether we write, draw, paint, or scrapbook, the results will be in front of us as a reminder of how bad we *think* we are. Unfortunately, this keeps some from ever getting started with a creative outlet. If you learn nothing else from lessons in the sand, please take to heart that paper, canvas, or any other medium for that matter, can be hidden, ripped up, scribbled over, thrown out, and even burned . . . just as quickly as the sand can be obliterated when the results don't meet with our expectations. Pen, paper, paint, or canvas are not our enemies, or something to fear because of their lasting qualities; they are simply the means to an end. If the result of our efforts is not worthy by our standards, we must be willing to set it aside or throw it away and start anew. Creative skills increase with practice and, with practice, improvements are inevitable.

The need for perfection is like driving through life with the emergency brake on, often causing unnecessary damage. Desiring to succeed is one thing, but the unrelenting constraint of striving for excellence sometimes holds back true ability from expressing itself. Just today, a seven-year-old boy told me he does really well at tee-ball when his dad's not there. It's sad when anxiety starts at such a young age and yet so many carry this kind of mind-set with them through life. When the pressure is off, we naturally do better. It's as if the intimidation factor disappears and confidence gains momentum, allowing our talents to develop at an appropriate pace.

Sand is not daunting because it has no lasting power and leaves no memory of any sculpture, whether it was perfect or not. If the tide doesn't come in soon enough to wipe out a mistake or a poor design, it can easily be trampled under foot. Because of this, ample creative energy goes into this artistic endeavor. While working with sand, stress and restraint don't seem relevant. Even people who don't feel artistically inclined can join in and have a good time because there are no *lasting* expectations . . . just creative fun.

Another great motivator of sand art is that you can keep adding to it; there are no limitations. Once, we shaped two dolphins coming up out of the water, gracefully tipping their heads, looking majestic as dolphins often do. We added some waves around them and thought we were done. Then our son Stephen, who wasn't tired of it yet, started heaping sand up a short distance behind the dolphins. When we asked what he was doing, he only replied, "You will have to wait and see." As our curiosity peaked, up out of the sand came "Jaws" pursuing the dolphins. How it changed the whole mood by adding suspense. It was a creative moment we all enjoyed.

Sand art not only brings pleasure to the one creating it, it captures the attention of those passing by. One of the most gratifying moments after hours of digging and shaping sand is to have admirers pause to look at what we've made. Some look quickly and move on, while others stop, taking the time to appreciate our handiwork and strike up a conversation.

Once, our family spent hours sculpting a large lion with a huge mane. It was late in the day when we finished and the beach was clearing, except for those who were out for an evening walk. Many stopped to look and commented on a "job well done." After a bit, we moved away from the lion to watch from a distance how people would respond as they passed. Just about every person that went by stopped to look more closely and most of their expressions reflected some kind of contemplation. We couldn't tell what they were thinking, nor did it matter. The important result was a visual experience worth the pause in their walk along the beach.

Developing Talent

As you ponder these points, keep in mind that all creative endeavors can be experienced in much the same way as working with sand. They have no lasting value until you complete something you really like and choose to make permanent. Come prepared to invest time and effort into developing your skills; but also realize it's acceptable to let *the tide* wash away disappointments, such as imperfect results from your early attempts. Activating this *discard if needed* approach will bring a new level of freedom. Try it for yourself and see.

It's improbable to think our first piece of art will be a masterpiece, no matter what the medium. That same masterpiece, however, will never come into being without a willingness to develop our talents one new *surface* at a time. When success does come, it's a feeling that cannot be matched, especially if we've learned to enjoy the process. Don't allow lofty goals to deprive you of the immediate pleasure that results from participating in creative activities. Experiencing victory can only become a reality when there's something to conquer, and at times, this involves taking risks. Goodyear, Edison, and Bell tried many things and met with many setbacks before each produced some of our most useful inventions. The world is a better place because people throughout the ages dared to express themselves and put their creative ideas to use. Adventurous and risk-taking artisans have left us a written, visual, and musical history, beckoning us to follow. May we faithfully pursue by overcoming our fears and leave an artistic legacy of our own.

It's liberating to realize our less-than-impressive creative endeavors can brighten someone's day. Our family isn't very skilled at making sand sculptures compared with many, yet people still take the time to look and enjoy, because we took the time to create. This holds true for any artistic medium, including music, crafts, gardening, baking or any other hobby you enjoy. People like art, all kinds of art, and when we're creative, the world is a better place because of it.

In conclusion, consider the tide—it turns, and so do our creative opportunities. Let's not miss our chance because we didn't dare to try. Don't hide behind the clichés of "I can't . . ." or "I'm not artistic." If need be, take a trip to the beach and have some good creative fun in the sand. While there, proclaim, "I can . . ." "I am . . ." "I will put my heart and my hands to an artistic project and stick with it long enough to discover the creative side of me really does exist."

The next chapter will help us understand this *creative process*. It will instruct us how to reach a place where we can experience creative fulfillment.

chapter three
finding creative fulfillment

To everything there is a season, a time for every
purpose under heaven. Ecclesiastes 3:1

Have you ever wished you could be in two places at once? How about wanting to reach your destination without having to travel? Poof—instantly there! I'm sure most of us have at least entertained the thought and we don't stop there, often wanting to accomplish things immediately, too. We can easily frustrate ourselves though, by trying to live outside the realm and reality of God's purposes. This chapter will help us understand our creative limitations and how to work with them as well as through them.

God ordained the principal of circumscription at the beginning of creation; establishing boundaries for every situation and circumstance we encounter. When He made the world, it was perfect. Man was, too. Yet, even in this state of perfection, man's view of the world was still limited to his immediate surroundings, the Garden of Eden.

From here, he gazed toward heaven and beheld the sun, moon, and stars, gaining only a glimpse of the universe of which he had become a part.

God could have created our world all at once; but He chose to put it together in steps; note the Days of Creation found in Genesis 1. Following this prototype, He doesn't usually allow us to skip the process, simply to gain results. That's why we are limited to one artistic expression at a time. God made it so our creative desires and accomplishments would take time and energy. They would require thought and growth, but most importantly and to our benefit, they should fill a lifetime. We cannot communicate all the creative ability within us through one story, poem, song, painting, dance, craft, quilt . . . It will take many expressions, according to the pattern God set; it's also encouraging to know our creative course will change and improve as we grow and mature. There are no shortcuts—plain and simple, everything about creativity is a process.

We have the ability to observe with our five senses, the capacity to think and take action, and the wherewithal to be innovative and expressive. The creative experience is available to each one of us, but forced upon none. The choice is ours whether or not to begin this journey. Once we do, the place we start will not be the place we end. As we apply ourselves to use and develop the talents God has given us, we will find it's not about reaching a destination, but about benefiting from the means whereby we expand our horizons . . . yet never completely arriving.

Human nature wants immediate gratification; fast food restaurants have ample business because they can quickly satisfy our hunger. Many like to buy things on credit so they don't have to wait until they can afford them. This kind of thinking spills into craving instant success or getting rich quick. It makes life all about us and our needs, but God doesn't see it this way and His timetable doesn't generally align with ours, either. He's never in a hurry, and He always has something for us to learn, accomplish, or overcome along the way.

Therefore, the pace at which we develop creative abilities won't discourage us once we understand the process is a good portion of God's purpose for our lives.

Accomplishments are not the only thing life is about. Taking part in an activity can be just as invigorating as the outcome. If we always put our expectations or satisfaction off until the finished product and promising results are obtained, it leaves for little pleasure along life's way—even when success comes. This reminds me of the year our oldest daughter, Karen, played on a winning high school soccer team. First, they won their own Sectional Title and the Western Regional Qualifier to make the State Tournament. They then moved on to the semi-finals and, ultimately, the New York State Championship, which they won. Now you would think the results would have been exhilarating, and I suppose, for a short time, they were. Nevertheless, it wasn't long before I heard people on the sidelines saying, "In a way it's disappointing because there are no more games." No more process. Even some of the players said they were surprised they felt a "let-down" because it was over. Don't get me wrong; the results were exciting and the players and fans were thrilled. The team had won it all and everyone was extremely happy and proud of them for capturing the title. Yet in actuality, the long practices, overcoming injuries, hard work, tough games, tears, and triumphs, throughout the season were very rewarding. These things, in themselves, brought great satisfaction. There was also a strong sense of camaraderie and care developed one for another on the long road to their common goal. The process will forever be a significant part of their memories when they think about winning States.

A Process–Not an Event

David is a professional landscaper and extremely talented. A few years ago, he was asked to take the position of Master Gardener at a large estate. The new owner gave David a general idea of what he was looking for and left the details up to him. After accepting the job, David set out to make the property beautiful. Trees and shrubs were planted and a large waterfall with lily ponds was added, along with a great variety of exotic flowers. Attractive rock pathways adorned the grounds and the grandeur of the estate was improving nicely.

Then one day, as the owner took a stroll around his property with David, he seemed disappointed. Noticing this, David inquired of the problem. "It doesn't look finished, I expected more," was the owner's reply.

David understood his frustration, but also knew he was on track to achieving the results he wanted. "Gardening is a process, not an event," he encouraged. "It takes time for the trees and shrubs to grow filling in the bare spots, for the plants to become hearty and full. Give it time and you will have just what you've been looking for."

Thinking about this, I realize David's statement is true regarding anything we deem important or precious, creativity not excluded. Yes, like the owner of this large estate, we all want results and most of us want them right away; but creative fulfillment will only come when we learn to enjoy the process and grow with it.

Terri longs to be a successful artist. She has taken several drawing and painting classes and faithfully works on her art at home. After seeing her latest painting, I mentioned how nicely it turned out. Her response, "Maybe in a few years and after a lot more classes, I'll be good." The tone of her voice made me wonder if she was having any fun at becoming an artist.

"The important thing is that you enjoy the process," I replied.

Her tone changed and a smile rolled across her face as she said, "Oh, but I do."

Yet, it was then Terri realized her resolve to succeed occasionally interfered with how she really felt. Have you ever found yourself in a similar situation, where the prospect of greatness consumed you? We must be careful not to become so pre-occupied with the outcome that we forget God designed the process with a purpose in mind.

Results are important, even necessary. They give us a sense of accomplishment and a platform whereby we can be heard; but it doesn't begin or end there for the artist. When success comes, it's only a part of the equation, a piece of the puzzle, a glimpse of the vast resource within each one of us. Once we finish a piece of art, a quilt, a poem, a song, the purpose isn't merely to be impressed by what we've produced and then quit. Instead, the finished product beckons us to initiate a new one. The same holds true for dancers, musicians, and other artisans; we willingly participate because of a passion for our creative expression, acknowledging practice takes much longer than performing. Moreover, the success of our performance depends upon our preparation. Ultimately, the moment of applause won't seem worth it, if the process doesn't satisfy.

Creative activity will not always be enjoyable, there may even be times of real frustration; but it shouldn't be on a continual basis. The attitude whereby we approach a medium will determine the level of pleasure and success. Compare this with people who are emotionally strong; when they encounter hardships, they persevere, grow in character and feel good about overcoming. The creative will do the same once determination and patience prevail. The owner of the large estate had visions of grandeur and was determined to get what he wanted; but he didn't have a realistic comprehension of the process, which brought about the previously mentioned disappointment. By changing his outlook, he learned to enjoy each season of growth, watching for improvements that only time could bring. It's important to keep our goals in perspective and not lose heart when things don't go as planned, or if they take longer than expected. Think about it, every mighty oak starts as a sapling in the shadows of greatness. The process is where results are formed—enjoy it.

Allow Time to Grow

Once, while teaching a watercolor course, I forgot to tell my students there would be an Art Show held at the conclusion of these lessons. I remembered the week before our last class and told my students I would need to collect a painting from each of them next week. "What?" they responded. "No one told us we had to put our work on display." One even went so far as to say, "I wouldn't have taken this class if I knew I had to show my work."

I should point out this was a *beginners'* class and these people had never painted before; they were simply looking for a creative outlet. They took the class to see if watercolor might be fun, not to draw attention to themselves. I spent the next few minutes trying to calm them down. The only thing that seemed to work was telling them I wouldn't collect anything, so not to worry about it. Next thing I knew, they were all back happily painting. This seemed rather drastic to me, but then I realized the pressure was off. These people wanted to do art for a hobby, not for a show. For them, it didn't seem feasible to put their work on display after only seven weeks of simple washes and painting techniques.

At first, their sense of panic surprised me, but then it is human nature to want to be impressive at whatever we do. We may want to put our work in a show "once we are good," but not while we're learning. Fear becomes a factor in situations like this and suddenly our level of skill undermines action. These students were fine in the privacy of a classroom; creativity flowed, ability increased, and everyone was having a good time, but the thought of a public show intimidated them, threatening their creative futures.

This scenario offers two lessons. First, for those of us who teach or promote the arts, we must not scare off potential artists with undue pressure. When encouraging creative outlets, or developing new talent, we must take into consideration the personalities and expectations of our students. Not all beginners will feel the same way, but in this class, not one of them wanted to be in the exhibition. Therefore, we must be sensitive to individual needs and allow for personal growth. The goal should be to help our students become secure in their abilities before expecting them to perform on a public level.

The second lesson is for new artists. The show was not meant to embarrass anyone. The class description clearly stated a *beginner's watercolor class*. For that matter, all the different classes represented were for beginners. Shows like these are set up to build confidence and give you an opportunity to meet other artists. If you find yourself in this kind of situation, step back and look at your art, see what you've accomplished and be encouraged to continue. Keep in mind, this is only the beginning; each creative action from this point forward will only improve. In time, you could draw or paint to decorate your home, or give your artwork as gifts. You may eventually enter your art in juried shows, and perhaps even sell your work in galleries. The choice is yours as to how far you will go with developing your talent. But in the meantime, don't let what you consider a very bad first painting or drawing keep you from the process of showing your work to others and more importantly, from doing art at all. And please, don't let one little show prevent you from taking a class, no matter what your creative outlet.

A month passed before I was reminded that I needed to collect a painting from every one who took my class. Therefore, I called each student to see if he/she would be willing at this point to submit a painting for the art show. To my surprise and great pleasure, they *all* brought something. Some even brought paintings they had done since the class. Finally, the night for the Open House came—there were four different classes represented. The room overflowed with smiling faces and family members who came to support and enjoy the exhibit. A sense of accomplishment filled the air and the outcome was amazing. During the class, none of them wanted to deal with the pressure of a show; but now that the class was over and they had a chance to look back at what they had achieved, they were ready for their *first* results. This show actually encouraged these new artists to take more classes and continue the process toward a lifetime of creative fulfillment.

Setting Realistic Goals

Are you one that has said, "I can't" before ever attempting a creative project? You just might be surprised at the ability within you, if you would simply put forth some effort. On the other hand, maybe you tried, but quit too quickly. Often, the adjustment can be made by moving your motivation from your head to your heart, and from fearing the outcome to taking pleasure in the process. It's amazing how many people feel inadequate. Some are dealing with issues of insecurity, while others only do things they are confident they can do well. Consequently, if they are not sure of the results, they may find it easier to believe they can't do it and simply not bother trying. This kind of thinking keeps people from experiencing life to the fullest and from productively using the gifts God has given them.

Often the "I can't" people don't create because of this consuming factor: it won't be good enough. Amber told me she liked to do crafts, but didn't work on them very often because she was "afraid of failure." Even though she enjoyed working on crafts, she was never pleased with the finished product. Then I discovered an underlying problem: her dissatisfaction came from comparing her projects with those of her aunt, who happened to be a *seasoned pro*. She was intimidated because of the relationship and this paralyzed her ability to enjoy the process. The result? She quit trying to be creative at all. What's sad about this story is that Amber's aunt never criticized her crafts or made her feel incapable—she came up with these thoughts all by herself. This unrealistic comparison of abilities crippled Amber's desire and stole her opportunity to find creative fulfillment. How unfortunate when we lock our own creative doors, tormented by pressures that don't exist.

Then there's Frank. He called to let me know he wouldn't be at the next watercolor class. Inquiring why, he declared, "Because painting is too frustrating!" *Frustrating* seemed a bit severe, seeing he had only used his paints a few times. What, then, was Frank's problem? He set his expectations extremely high and anticipated mastering the process immediately. When this didn't happen, he became disillusioned and quit. Part of the problem was that a friend invited him to come to a painting class where the other artists were experienced and already doing quality work. He hadn't considered the fact that they had all been painting for some time and he was only just beginning. Nor did he understand that finding creative fulfillment and being pleased with the outcome could, at times, be two very different things. Some are thrilled to see improvements every time they paint and the process carries them. Others are only pleased if they meet certain criteria and often end up begrudging the time and effort it takes to develop their talent.

Expecting too much too quickly usually deters us from continuing, especially when discouragement overshadows reality. If we lose sight of our purpose for wanting to be creative in the first place, it makes it hard to give our ability a fair chance to prosper. This can result in hours of lost creative expression and pleasure, all because our initial expectations were excessive. There's nothing wrong with wanting to do a thing well; we just need to make sure we provide ample time for growth and improvement. Each of us will progress at a different pace. The secret is allowing the experience to meet that creative need even *before* reaching the intended goal. This will actually increase our opportunities to succeed and, even if the desired mark is never reached in skill, the process can still satisfy.

Keep in mind, when comparing skills, the longer a person actively participates in their form of art, the more proficient they become. Do you think famous artists are at the same level of ability as they were when they first began? Not a chance. Even those with a good amount of natural talent realize the more time they spend honing their skills, the better they become. Improving at anything we do in life takes time, effort, and a good attitude; God created it to be so.

Here are a few questions you can ask yourself before getting started.

☞ *What is my motive?*

☞ *Why do I put such high expectations on my abilities before giving them a fair chance to develop?*

☞ *Does my fulfillment depend upon the approval or praise of others? (More about this in Chapter Fourteen.)*

The fact of the matter is, artistic endeavors can simply be enjoyable and fulfilling, even if we never become famous or receive recognition.

Milestones or Steppingstones?

With each generation, it seems more people gauge the meaningfulness of their lives by their accomplishments, rather than by their experiences that obtained them. Significant events automatically mark life, such as our first words, our first day of school, graduation, marriage, and so forth throughout our lives. We call these events milestones, each important in its own right. However, we must not ignore the steppingstones, the day-to-day occurrences that get us from one point to the next. Milestones do not fill a lifetime. The majority of life lays in-between major events. For example, high school graduation marks a wonderful and commendable achievement, but for most of us, it took thirteen years or four thousand seven hundred and forty-five days to accomplish. Our education, family, teachers, friends, coaches, interesting experiences, challenges, good times and bad, all filled those days, weeks, months, and years that made us the adults we've become. The diploma was a milestone; the process taught us how to live.

Creative fulfillment builds on translating simple actions into everyday results. These actions may not be notable by themselves, but the result can never be noteworthy without them. Do we expect a newborn baby to walk? Do we assume a six-month-old should be able to talk in complete sentences? Of course not. These things are a part of the natural growth process; and remember, it's not an event. As children grow, we expect them to progress toward maturity. Accordingly, how can we expect our newborn creative desire to perform at levels beyond what's realistic? Why do we think we should be able to skip childhood and be all grown up on our first creative attempt? Why do we trick ourselves into believing we should be as good as someone that has years more experience? These kinds of attitudes hinder creative growth and fulfillment.

We are created to be creative, but there has to be a beginning and the fact that this beginning may not be very spectacular is merely a part of the journey. This is comparable to children learning multiplication tables. They may feel overwhelmed at first, but in time, they brag about how easy it is. With practice, creative outlets become second nature, like riding a bike. Keep things in perspective, though. If you've put forth ample effort toward a certain creative endeavor and you can't seem to master it, don't quit—simply try something else, until you find one suitable to your personality and within the realm of your abilities.

We cannot shy away from participating just because we may not catch on as quickly as others, or because we don't feel we can live up to the expectations of those who have no patience. Often, the ones who must work more diligently at accomplishing their goals are farther ahead because of it. The process taught them to persevere and the results made them stronger. My son, Stephen, was quite shy when he was younger and *not* a standout athlete on the youth teams or in middle school. Nevertheless, he worked on his skills and became one of the best athletes in his high school. If discouraged by his less-than-great performance when he was younger, he could have given up. Instead, he worked through his weaknesses to become good at something he enjoyed.

This brought benefits to Stephen in other areas of life, as well. For example, he is not as shy as he used to be. Stephen also took up the guitar and plays well; even though I cannot say it was a pleasure to hear him during the first few months when many a poorly played chord filled our home. Nevertheless, through his determination and practice came ability. Now he enjoys the process and is pleased with the results—life doesn't get better than this.

Reflections of Who We Are

The sooner we start any endeavor, the more it shapes our future and brings with it additional opportunities for success. If some of you are older and have only recently desired or finally found the time for a creative outlet, don't lose heart; just be willing to work with what you have. Try not to pre-determine where you want to be and how quickly you want to get there, as it may take longer than you anticipate. Furthermore, we all need to take into consideration that our personalities will naturally show up in our creative outlets and, for this reason, we shouldn't expect our art to look or sound different from us.

Recently, I heard an elderly woman make a comment I thought to be humorous and yet, at the same time, revelatory. She said, "I have spent my whole life trying to be precise and, now that I'm trying to loosen up, I'm having a personality conflict." Eleanor made this remark while working on a painting she hoped would be much more relaxed in style. There was nothing wrong with the way she was used to painting, but she was looking for a change and found it harder than expected. Eleanor works toward perfection with everything she does, so it's not surprising this characteristic dominated her style of art. The fight was not with her paint; it was with her personality. I know how she feels because no matter how many times I've tried to loosen up a painting, it always ends up tight. But then, I like detail and I've learned to go with what works for me.

A point worth making here: none of us are going to revamp a lifetime of personality overnight, but adjustments can be made when deemed important—they just may take a while to accomplish or to be made permanent. We need to decide if changing our style or other behaviors is worth the effort, or if it's more advantageous to work with our natural instincts. What many of us don't realize is that drastic alterations to our creative outlets will bring about changes on a personal level, making a difference internally as well as in our art. Consequently, we should consider our cause, and ask ourselves if the change is necessary. Will it make for better results . . . all the way around? What's the ultimate goal? Wanting to improve our abilities or add vitality to our lives is a good thing, but pursuing change simply for the sake of change is not necessarily beneficial, nor will it be easy.

As we move on to the next chapter, let's keep in mind that artistic actions simply reflect one's identity. If the art changes (for any length of time), so will the artist. If the artist changes, so will the art—the two are inseparable and more evidence of the fact that God made us unique. Understanding this concept improves our chances of finding creative fulfillment.

chapter four

choosing a creative outlet

In all your ways acknowledge Him, and He
shall direct your paths. Proverbs 3:6

Artistic avenues build confidence, bringing excellent opportunities for individual expression. Removing the masks of insecurities and the need for approval by accepting God's sovereign design for our lives are the first steps. The rest is simply a matter of taking action to improve the skills He has so graciously given. Don't be surprised when you find your confidence growing in other areas of life as well, because the arts possess influence beyond our creative resources. For example, people who exhibit boldness with a paintbrush are usually extroverted. If you're not as outgoing as you would like, you can work on being more expressive within the privacy of your creative outlet. Try experimenting with different techniques, take risks, and don't worry about whether any of it meets with your expectations, because that's not the emphasis of this exercise. Sometimes participation alone can revolutionize your approach. Courage to attempt new things increases with each experience, which also allows for personal growth as your artistic abilities develop.

I'm not talking about a miraculous transformation. Changes will occur at varying intervals as individuality dictates. The degree of determination toward accomplishing our objectives makes a difference as well. Be attentive in recognizing limitations and take care not to tackle things outside God's purpose for your life. Be honest with yourself about what you can and cannot do. Sometimes people chase after specific talents—not because they're gifted in that area, but because they think it will make them popular or more impressive in the eyes of others. This purpose does not represent the heart of God nor should it be our source of motivation. We may not have the talents we *want*, but when we discover the talents we *have* and use them accordingly, contentment comes. From here, we have the opportunity for our creative outlet to bless those it reaches. One goal for this book is to help each of you understand that God not only created us as individuals, He created us with purpose and has given us the abilities needed to fulfill that purpose.

Aubrey had a fascination with theater and often thought about becoming a famous actress. Yet, she met with disappointment on several occasions when not chosen for a major role in any of the plays for which she auditioned. Why was this? She did not have the strong stage presence needed for acting and her voice wavered. However, she does have a creative mind and the ability to write well. Accepting this, Aubrey now works toward becoming a playwright, thankful for a way to stay involved with her dream. Her desire for theatrical involvement led her in the right direction, but her talent developed through a different *role* than she had envisioned.

If you have a passion for a specific art, but it doesn't seem attainable, pray. Ask God to show you if this desire is of Him, or if it's a distraction to keep you from your true purpose. Once you have your answer, take appropriate action. Aubrey was on the right road, but driving the wrong vehicle. When the adjustment came, so did creative fulfillment.

Discovering Talents

Often people's artistic abilities remain unused because they never took time to discover what skills come naturally to them. Not long ago, I sat in on a home school drawing class, where twenty-two students, ranging in age from six to sixteen, participated. While there, I noticed Lori, one of the parents, took up a drawing board and began to sketch along with the children. Glancing over at her paper, I was pleased to see she had talent; she even took the initiative to add the appropriate shading and made her objects look real. At the end of class, she made the comment, "I didn't know I could draw," as she smiled triumphantly. Lori didn't realize she could draw because she had never tried.

Another factor to consider: we don't have to know exactly what our abilities are before choosing a creative outlet. We can compare this venture with high school seniors deciding on a career path. There is no hurry or need to make that decision before graduating because the majority of college students change their major at least once. Accordingly, if we are unsure of our creative likes or abilities, we can experiment with the options. We may not discover an interest in something until we've spent some time and effort on a specific art. Gary took up oil painting in his late thirties and he was amazed how quickly his skills developed. Until then, he had no idea how much talent he possessed. I do want to point out however, that he first started painting with watercolors, but that medium did not suit his personality. Thankfully, Gary stuck with the process long enough to see his ability blossom when he switched to oils.

There is no rule that dictates how many creative outlets we can have. I enjoy three or four different things on a regular basis, along with a few others that, from time to time, catch my attention. I'm not the only one multi-tasking either. Recently, I attended a local art show and noticed that several artists used a different medium for each piece they submitted. Some of these artists have an eclectic collection of things they like to do, while others simply haven't decided upon which medium they prefer. Therefore, they are looking at, and working with, different options. Either way, they are engaging in creative activity.

Linda came to the place in her life where she wanted a creative outlet. First, she took a drawing class and enjoyed it, but wasn't convinced this medium was for her. Next, she took a watercolor class. Although she liked learning the techniques and socializing with other artists, this didn't excite her, either. Amazingly, Linda didn't lose heart. She told me she was going to try the saxophone next and, if that didn't work, she would look for something else.

I appreciate Linda's attitude. Here we have a woman in her early fifties yearning to find the perfect way to express the creative awakening that recently surfaced. She is very determined and willing to try different things; but, even more importantly, she is able to let go of what doesn't work and eagerly starts something new. Because of a delay in working out a time for saxophone lessons, Linda told me she took some *tole* painting classes and loved it. She found her creative outlet. Thank God, she didn't give up after her first, or even second, venture. In addition, during the drawing and watercolor classes, she acquired skills that would be helpful in tole painting. All things really do work together for good.

It's fun discovering what ignites an interest, especially when we're not intimidated to explore the vast range of possibilities. If it works, we are better because of it. If not, after putting forth some honest effort, there's no harm deciding that's not for me. Be willing to try different things to see what brings the most satisfaction. Keep in mind, the *best* outlet for us doesn't always have to be what we can do the best, because great results may not come for a while. The best might simply be the added vitality gained from doing something creative and enjoying the process.

If you aren't as good as you want to be, especially at the beginning, it can still be fun. The pivotal point in any endeavor hangs upon our ability to keep things in perspective. If we stay optimistic, improvements will inevitably come.

When our oldest daughter, Karen, went to college, she ran track because some of her closest friends did. She never won a race, or even came close for that matter; but she learned very early in the season not to put unrealistic expectations on her own ability. She realized this was all new to her and that she was running against people with a lot more experience. Consequently, winning wasn't the goal; improving race times was. Because of her positive attitude and strong work ethic, satisfaction came in the form of personal victories. This same approach works wonders when applied to the arts.

Now that we understand the creative life is attainable, we must take action as soon as possible; otherwise, this fresh stirring toward the arts will dissipate and lose its appeal. Some of you may be thinking, "I have the desire, but I don't know where to start." If this is the case, here are a few ideas to get your creative journey under way.

Journaling

Because of individuality, the quest for the right outlet will vary; however, keeping a journal is one creative outlet that can benefit all who try it. Most can deal with the prospect of keeping a journal because no one else has to read it and personal expression has full reign within its pages. Depending upon your view of creativity, your journal entries might start with "I can't..." "I'm afraid..." or "I don't know..." Then the more you write, you might find yourself recording disappointments or past hurts and thus, it may not seem like a constructive outlet at first. But, in time, if you will write at least a little every day, you will find your words turning to positive goals and discovering hidden dreams. Writing has the power to stretch our thinking beyond the immediate, the obvious, and the mundane.

Mandy's job was time consuming and stressful. Because of this, she felt uninspired and exhausted. In view of her situation, I asked if she had ever considered a creative outlet—something to help clear her mind and turn her focus back to the Lord, where she could find inner peace. She had not, and was adamant about not having any creative abilities. Taking into account Mandy's disposition and her frustration with work, I suggested she start a journal. It doesn't have to be time consuming and it's a good channel for releasing emotions. She agreed to try it. About a month later, I asked Mandy if the journal entries had helped to relieve any stress. Again, the answer was no. I didn't expect this response, but then discovered there was no journal.

Shortly afterward, Mandy's place of employment required her to take a college level Creative Writing course. God put her in a situation that forced her to write and through this experience, she found writing to be a positive outlet. The last time I spoke with Mandy, she said she had started a journal and it not only helped reduce stress, it improved her outlook toward faith, family, and the things that truly are important to her. What a noticeable difference this simple creative outlet made. Hope returned and even her countenance brightened.

Words influence our thoughts and consequently our future. Proverbs 18:21 puts it this way, "Death and life are in the power of the tongue, and those who love it will eat its fruit." One of our goals should be to encourage a positive point of view through our journal. Have you ever noticed that many of the Psalms start with a discouraged tone, a cry for help; but by the end of each, there is hope and praise to God? Psalm 69:29–30 says, "But I am poor and sorrowful; Let Your salvation, O God, set me up on high. I will praise the name of God with a song, and will magnify Him with thanksgiving." David understood his praise did not make the Almighty any bigger and yet he could ward off fear and doubt by magnifying the Lord and acknowledging God's sovereignty in every situation. We can accomplish this through a journal. When we write with our Creator in mind, even disappointments take on new meaning and attitudes can be kept in check. In addition, as we search for the exact words of expression, our thinking has a chance to line up with God's will.

From here, you can write about anything and everything. Try mixing things up a bit; journal entries don't always have to be about your day or what you're going through. If you like keeping a daily record, buy a second notebook and use it for writing short stories, poems, and even an occasional joke just for fun. Watch how your writing improves, while sparking fresh enthusiasm. Before you know it, optimistic words will flow out of your heart and onto the pages. If this is not the case, pray and ask God to help you to see things through His eyes. Life is a gift; seeing it for what it is makes all that we go through worthwhile.

It's difficult to write about hopes and dreams without thinking of ways to fulfill them. There were several times while working on this book that I wanted to quit right where I was and go paint. I remember one time in particular I had to laugh, thinking, "I'm even inspiring myself to do art." Writing about the arts ignited my passion for creative activity and the power of my own words cheered me on. Writing down your goals can help move you to action.

Just because we begin a journal, doesn't mean we have to commit to becoming an author, or feel obligated to try other innovative things. We are all different and have various levels of creative desire; for some a journal will be enough, for others it will merely be a starting point. Either way, it's a powerful outlet that can benefit all who heed the call to write—thinking about it just won't do. Many people dream of greatness, but only those who put forth the effort have the opportunity to succeed.

Poetry

Writing poetry is another stimulating activity; it promotes reflective thought, increases vocabulary, and helps us articulate heart-felt emotion. Many shy away from traditional arts such as drawing, painting, or playing an instrument for fear of open scrutiny. Poetry, on the other hand, can be kept private until you are ready to venture out into the public arena. For me, writing poetry is a means to express feelings that need an outlet but not necessarily an audience. Occasionally, a poem works to the point where I think someone else would gain from its insight, so then I'll share it; but even if no one ever read a poem I've written, it still did something for me, the process itself gratifies.

If you choose to write poetry, approach it with the idea of growth. Start on a personal level and don't set unrealistic deadlines for success. Also, take into consideration it could be the very tool God has given you to share with others. Later in this book, we will learn how to apply these principles to our lives, and how to minister to others through our creative outlets. We will also see how God's purpose always goes beyond us.

Singing

Everyone can enjoy singing. "My lips shall greatly rejoice when I sing to You, and my soul, which You have redeemed" (Psalm 71:23). We are not limited to the lyrics or tunes of others, either. We can "sing to the LORD a new song! Sing to the LORD, all the earth" (Psalm 96:1). Even if it doesn't sound professional, freedom of expression exists as we lift our voice in song.

In Exodus 15, Moses and the children of Israel sang a song of praise to God for safe passage through the Red Sea and for destroying Pharaoh's army. A song seemed fitting to express their appreciation to God for all the great and marvelous things He had done.

In 1 Samuel 1, we find Hannah unable to conceive and, to make matters worse, she had a rival daily reminding her of this fact. Many years passed before God answered her petition for a son. At Samuel's birth, Hannah was so thankful she burst forth in song; it's recorded in 1 Samuel 2:1–10.

Music is an excellent outlet for affection. Love songs fill the airwaves because passionate lyrics resonate well when put to music. Jubilant songs cause us to celebrate or rejoice. Sad songs make us sympathetic toward loss or sacrifice. Patriotic songs promote national pride.

Music contains diversity in sound, style, and lyrics, making it easy for all to join in, at least to some extent. Even if some of you don't think you can sing very well, God made room for all of us in "Make a joyful shout to the LORD, all you lands! Serve the LORD with gladness; come before His presence with singing" (Psalm 100:1–2). Ephesians 5:19 encourages, "Speaking to one another in psalms and hymns and spiritual songs, singing and making melody in your heart to the Lord." James 5:13 admonishes, "Is anyone among you suffering? Let him pray. Is anyone cheerful? Let him sing psalms." "It is good to give thanks to the LORD, and to sing praises to Your name, O Most High" (Psalm 92:1). Singing evokes creative flow; and who knows, some of you may discover you have an incredible voice and should share your talent with others.

Sketchbook

Sketchbooks are a lot of fun. They come in several sizes, so it's easy to keep one near by. Again, we don't have to show our sketchbook to anyone, which gives us opportunity to try different techniques and get comfortable with a pencil. Like anything in life, the more we do something, the more we will improve, and the easier it will become. If serious or realistic sketching doesn't work, we can try calligraphy, caricatures, or abstract drawing; even doodling on scrap paper helps. My daughter, Jessica, had the nickname of "Doodling Jay" in school because she was always drawing something. I love it because when I need a card made, some lettering done or a quick drawing for a project, she can do a nice job without hesitation. She is the one who did the chapter graphics for this book.

Unfortunately, when I was in high school, I learned to *graph* everything, which drastically limited my freehand drawing skills, as well as restricting my ability to be spontaneous and expressive. I've done some sketching recently and found it particularly enjoyable when I'm in the mood to relax. Without applying much effort, this no-pressure approach has already improved my artistic touch and is noticeable in my most recent works of art. Here I've practiced my own preaching and found it beneficial. If we can draw well, it makes it easier to do layouts and shading techniques for several different kinds of art.

No matter where you choose to start, creative outlets don't have to be time consuming or performance oriented. They can be simple bursts of musical expression, poetic verse, written thoughts, or spontaneous sketching. Each is an excellent outlet for alleviating stress, filling voids, and bringing pleasure. They can be a daily exercise or an occasional resting place. We can choose one or do them all, but the bottom line: it's all about getting started, discovering our abilities and taking our talents seriously. We should also take into account the amount of creative activity needed to keep us mentally and emotionally refreshed. That amount will be different for each of us; but bear in mind, many a famous author, poet, songwriter, and artist got their start on a personal level with a piece of scrap paper and an idea.

Take an Art Class

Another great way to get started in the art of your choice is to take a class. Be ready to learn and willing to participate while allowing the teacher to lay the necessary groundwork. I see nothing wrong with approaching the sessions with great anticipation; this is usually a good motivator—just be wary of expecting immediate success. Unfortunately, this unrealistic attitude works against new artists. Trying to hurry creative skills often hinders or slows the process because the strain is too much. On one occasion, I had a woman rip her painting up and throw it in the trash, right during class. Her explanation? It wasn't any good. To say the least, she is *not* painting today.

There've been times when my watercolor students wanted to start a painting the first week of class. This was without going through the basic watercolor techniques necessary to understand how the paint works and some of the concepts needed to pull a painting together. Initially, I thought it ambitious and considered seeing how they would do, but then realized it would not be in *their* best interest. I could liken it to playing golf; it's a lot easier to learn how to swing a club correctly than to have to rectify bad habits. No matter what we want to excel at, we must first master the basics. (In advanced classes, I expect my students to take the initiative to start a painting and work at their own pace; but not on the first day of a beginner's class.) I needed to curb these students' eagerness and teach them that patiently mastering the fundamentals would make their painting abilities much stronger and drastically increase the probability of becoming great artists. And, believe it or not, we will meet our objectives much sooner when we don't take shortcuts.

In yet another class, a woman, who already knew how to paint with acrylics, started without any guidance, using watercolor in a very thick manner. It took some effort on my part to show her how the two kinds of paint worked differently. For her to fully appreciate the watercolor experience, she needed to use them like watercolors. Once she learned appropriate techniques, she would discover the method and effect quite different from acrylic. Then she could choose which of the two mediums she preferred and develop her talent in that direction. After several weeks of coaxing, this woman finally adjusted her approach and was able to paint in a style that reflected watercolor. Since then, she has taken other watercolor classes and has found the medium suits her well.

Learning how to use any medium correctly will eliminate some of the pitfalls and frustrations of trying to figure it out on our own. When taking a class, no matter what the course, we should come with a teachable attitude. The teacher not only knows when it's time to let us move ahead, but also can teach us some *tricks of the trade*, accelerating our progress. If a class you're interested in is not available in your area, buy a "How-To" book and commit to doing each exercise—no shortcuts!

Expanding Knowledge

I've attended classes where many of the students were experienced artists and I've thought, "Why in the world are they taking this course?" But then there's nothing so infectious as a room full of creative people excited about being creative. Dedicated artists keep their eyes and ears open to new ideas and recognize there are no limits to expanding their knowledge. They attend these classes to further their education and to soak in the creative environment. While there, they mingle with other artists, exchange ideas, and glean from each other's years of experience. Everyone gains.

Creative ability naturally increases when nurtured. If experienced artists understand this truth and continue to communicate with one another, we can all benefit from creative interaction. It's important to find people or take classes that motivate and challenge us to reach beyond our present skills.

Bill wanted a creative outlet, so he attended one of my painting classes. He learned quickly and was well on his way to becoming a fine artist. A few months after this, I saw Bill at a local store and asked him how his painting was coming along. Unfortunately, he had not touched his paints since our last class. He said it was hard for him to find time. Not long afterward, I taught another class and Bill was there. It wasn't that he didn't have the time; he just needed an incentive to make painting a priority. Having a set time and place to paint moved Bill to action.

Cecelia is another one who loves to do art, but seldom paints at home. She prefers taking classes and lives in an area where art courses are readily available. This motivates, challenges, and satisfies her creative desire. While Cecelia and others choose public gatherings, I would rather paint in the privacy of my own home. There is no set rule as to whether or not we should continue to take classes after we are comfortable with our medium. What's important is that we find what works for us and stick with it.

There is, however, one condition fundamental to all artistic growth—keeping a teachable attitude—no matter what our age or skill level. Romans 12:3 tells us, "For I say, through the grace given to me, to everyone who is among you, not to think of himself more highly than he ought to think, but to think soberly, as God has dealt to each one a measure of faith." If you ever reach the place where you feel you've arrived, I pray you will reconsider and realize this journey has no end, only higher heights, and new beginnings.

Exposing ourselves to new ideas and to other peoples' talents can propel our personal development beyond familiar horizons and keeps the process innovative. It opens doors to adventure and allows for experiences that might have otherwise been missed. I'm not suggesting we copy other's art, but rather filter ideas and concepts through our own unique personalities and patterns of thought. Each time we acquire a new skill or gain fresh insight, it helps to ensure well-rounded results. Proverbs 27:17 tells us, "As iron sharpens iron, so a man sharpens the countenance of his friend." This verse makes a strong case for constructive, yet challenging interaction. No matter what we want to improve upon, allowing other's expertise to rub off on us will make our ingenuity more effective.

If we isolate ourselves, eventually we'll run out of influential ideas. Have you ever noticed that some musicians' songs *all* sound alike? For me, they become boring and lose their appeal, along with their effectiveness. How about for you? Allowing outside participation could be the very component that keeps our work fresh and energetic. And being receptive to others doesn't have to be difficult, either. Even your pastor's sermons can initiate the inspiration for a new poem, song, or piece of art.

Maybe you're already a good artist, but seeking and accepting suggestions from time to time can make your art even better. Derrick, a watercolor artist, did a nice job of painting people but his flesh tones were flat, leaving a dull impression. Once he learned to use New Gamboge as an under wash, his flesh tones glowed, giving his paintings a more professional look. It was simply a matter of applying the advice given him, along with accepting the fact that there was room for improvement.

What many people don't understand is that Jesus has a plan for using our creative outlets to help accomplish His purpose in the earth. If we don't succeed at the arts, either because we never got started or we were unwilling to take advice and learn, we won't have the ability to use our talents for God's glory. Artistic endeavors usually begin on a personal level, activating the innate creative desire. But as skills improve, the platform changes and our talents have the opportunity to move outward, go public, and become a blessing to others. As we read on, we will learn how to make the most of this creative journey and how to acknowledge and take action with a higher purpose in mind. We must make ourselves available for the leading of the Holy Spirit

section two

be a doer and not a hearer only

hidden beauty

chapter five

a matter of priority

But he who looks into the perfect law of liberty and continues in it, and is not a forgetful hearer but a doer of the work, this one will be blessed in what he does. James 1:25

The more we incorporate creativity into our lives, the more we'll find ways to turn everyday activities into innovative ones. However, I want to focus for a moment on setting aside time specifically for the arts. Stop and consider; should finding or even making time for a creative outlet be a priority? I'm not asking if it should be the *top* priority, as if this were the only thing in life that can satisfy. Creativity should never take precedence over our relationship with Jesus Christ; nor should it come before legitimate responsibilities. Nevertheless, it can, and should be of consequence to us, seeing there are so many benefits, both to us personally and for those who will in time gain from our form of expression. Creativity on any level, be it observation, thinking, or action can positively affect our lives. If some of you have never had a creative outlet or let one slip away without regret, you may not understand the importance of finding the time to think and act creatively.

Distractions come in many forms, often occupying so much of the day that our creative nature does not have room to spread its wings and fly. Though desire naturally exists in each one of us, often other things simply crowd it out. When this happens, we could feel justified by what we've accomplished and have no regrets—not yet, anyway. In the future, we may look back on our lives and wish we had spent at least some of our time differently . . . creatively.

Most of our lives are extremely full; things to do, places to go, promotions to obtain, deadlines to meet, kids to raise, games to attend, church involvement, and community services to perform. Then at the end of a long hectic day, we want nothing more than to sit and do nothing for a while, knowing that tomorrow will be just as demanding. Our success driven culture dictates a good deal of our behaviors and this stretches most of us to our physical and emotional limits, leaving no time for creative pursuits. Consequently, time, or should I say, the *lack* thereof, is one of the biggest hindrances people have in becoming creative. I've heard many say, "When I retire, then I'll have time." Hopefully this will be true, but what about the lifetime in-between now and then? Not long ago, my husband and I were with a group of schoolteachers and one of them said, "Only two more years till I retire, then I'm going to play the organ and the piano and do all kinds of fun stuff." She was so excited about the prospect of unleashing her creative cravings. I thought, "Why wait?" Her kids are grown and gone, and she has the time now, if she would only make it a priority.

Then just today, I met a man who said he wanted to write a book, but just hadn't gotten around to it. He went on to say, "Maybe when I retire . . ." If we were all promised a long healthy life and our sunset years guaranteed, we could assure ourselves that someday we would enthusiastically pursue creative outlets. But we're not all promised a long and healthy life, and if we allow the cares of this world to consume us now, chances are we'll never see those sunset years at all, let alone enjoy them. Yes, we have responsibilities, things we cannot avoid; but continual labor with no time to relax can have adverse affects on us. Some are even dealing with health issues or problems in relationships because of it.

When someone or something is important to us, we adjust our schedules to make time. Why then do so many of us feel it's wrong to set aside a block of time to work on creative things? Releasing artistic expression increases our emotional and physical energy levels and helps rejuvenate our ability to meet responsibilities with a better attitude. We should never put our creative desire on a shelf, or keep it locked away within our souls, nor should we save it for a future date when we think we'll have the time. That time might never come.

Learning to Continue

My grandfather was a wonderful man with many talents. He had been an engineer; a missionary in Vellore, South India; and a College Professor. He loved music, was faithful to his church, active in his community, and extremely out-going.

With his health failing at the age of ninety-four, he came to live with my dad, where I visited him often. One afternoon I asked if he had any advice or lasting words of wisdom. His answer was short but reflective, "Don't ever stop doing something once you've started it." My grandfather built his life around discipline and routine. One of the things he did faithfully every day was play the piano. A skill he developed at a young age and, more importantly, something he continued right up to a few days before his death.

There would have been no purpose for his advice if it were always going to be easy. He learned through experience that the benefits of exercising a creative outlet far outweighed the time and effort put into maintaining such actions. He made it a priority, something he looked forward to.

Have you ever stopped doing something that once enhanced your life? Did circumstances, a lack of time, or even a waning of enthusiasm come between you and your creative pursuits? I used to play guitar and saxophone—skills developed, but not maintained. I'm not the only one facing this reality. Far too many people have told me, "I used to paint," "I used to play an instrument," "I used to keep a journal," etc. and it's always said with a bit of disappointment. Creative outlets require attention and a good level of commitment if they're going to remain a vital part of life. Things may come along that seem more meaningful to us at the time, but when we look back over the years, they won't necessarily be worth it. Once we stop actively doing something we previously enjoyed, we not only waste our talent, we nullify the positive outcome of such actions. 1 Corinthians 9:24–27 speaks about "running the race and finishing our course." There is no quitting the Christian walk until we meet Jesus face to face. Anything short of running this race for the rest of our lives is less than God's best for us. While here on earth, God has given us gifts and talents to help us run this race and it's to our benefit to use them. The Bible tells us David played the harp and was a worshiper long before he became a King. After David took the throne, he maintained his instrumental skills along with his time of worship; both contributed in making him the best King Israel ever had. Psalms exemplified his life, both in word and deed. "I will sing to the LORD as long as I live; I will sing praise to my God while I have my being" (Psalm 104:33). David understood the importance of keeping his creative outlet active, and how God used it to keep him strong even in times of great conflict.

In Acts 9:36–39 we find a woman named Dorcas who was "full of good works and charitable deeds." Her creative outlet was making coats and garments. When she died, her friends showed Peter some of the things she had made as a tribute to her. She used her talent to bring warmth and comfort to others. A lifetime of creative action was her testimony, even at the end.

Longevity and perseverance are crucial to anything we deem important. The race is not to the swift, but to those who endure. Creativity cannot take the place of salvation, but using the talents God has given us can certainly make life easier, more fruitful, and even more enjoyable. Most of us have a tendency to stick with the things we care about, therefore it truly is a matter of priority.

A Creative Break

A few years back, Colleen was doing her homework in my study. Distracted by a sudden commotion, I looked up to see her dancing happily around the room. After taking a few minutes to revel in the moment with her, I inquired to whether she had her homework done. It wasn't, so I jokingly asked, "Did you need a creative break?" Seriously, though, it was then I realized that she did need a break—from long division. Now that I think about it, she often dances with the music or she'll get out a microphone and sing along with her favorite songs. After a bit, she'll return to whatever she was doing, refreshed and ready to finish the task at hand.

Do you allow time for creative breaks? Have you ever stopped simply to enjoy the view? Listen to music? Read a poem? Thumb through an art, gardening, or home decorating magazine? It's amazing how a few minutes of interacting with something creative, or thinking about our next artistic project, revitalizes our mental and emotional energies. These actions actually enable us to return to our responsibilities more focused and with healthier attitudes. If we take this advice seriously, we will find our productivity improving at work or school. Some of us are stay-at-home moms with small children; short breaks increase our patience and can even help us think of innovative ways to involve the children in creative activities.

Refusing to slow down becomes a mental and physical snare. Fatigue sets in, numbs the senses, and causes us to overlook the creative moments that come our way. A world of good comes from taking time to observe, to hear, to feel, to dream, to live. Those who continually push themselves to the limit usually end up exhausted and miserable. Creative breaks—including meditation and worship—help us to keep things in perspective and to stay more in tune with our eternal purpose.

Creativity should be inspired, not forced, something to look forward to, not another obligation added to an already demanding schedule. Think of it as a place where the imagination can sore into a realm of endless possibilities and refreshing fun, a place we try to visit as often as possible.

A Foolish Vow

Active involvement in some form of creative action is an absolute must for me. My joy, strength, and service for Jesus depend upon it. I know this, because over seventeen years ago I purposely stopped painting. I had such a desire to see people accept Jesus into their lives that I made this *vow* to God, "I will not paint until someone gets saved." I loved to paint; therefore, I believed this sacrifice would move the heart of God. I was confident doors to witness would open without delay. Wrong. I was a stay at-home-mom and my children were little. There weren't a lot of opportunities to go out and save the world.

At that point in my life, I didn't understand the link between creativity and emotional health. I had no idea that not painting would cause such inner turmoil. Two long years passed and I had led no one to the saving grace of Jesus Christ. The result of putting my creative outlet aside became noticeable; my joy waned, I became restless, and I lost all confidence toward witnessing. My heart broke to think God wouldn't honor my sacrifice, and from my perspective, see people saved. What made things even worse, I saw no hope for opportunities to increase. I had already witnessed to all the people working at the local grocery store . . . with no success. Still, I would not break my vow and refused to pick up a paintbrush. By now, my mood swings were obvious and it was my husband, Ron, who made the connection between not painting and the change in my countenance. He suggested I start painting again. According to the scriptures, he could have released me from my vow, but I wasn't ready to quit. A few months later, Ron had had enough and made an appointment for us to talk with our Pastor about the vow and my not painting. Pastor told me straight out, "Arleen, you were wrong for making such a vow. It is good to have zeal and want to see people come to Jesus, but it's wrong to think you can move the hand of God by a self-inflicted, sacrificial vow." He helped me to understand that though my sacrifice was well intentioned and for a worthy cause, God never asked me to give up my art. I did this on my own, and in the end, it hurt my witness because I had no joy. By relinquishing my will to my husband's authority, and our Pastor's counsel, I was freed from this presumptuous vow. When we got home, I went straight to my studio, dusted off my desk, got out my supplies, and started a new painting . . . along with a new life.

To this day, if circumstances or busyness keeps me from a creative outlet for any length of time, I get restless. I've learned to keep a painting started in my studio and a quilt ready to work on in the family room. More recently, I find writing fills the void and I have a few projects on my computer; this way I always have something I can work on for as much time as I have or want.

Now you may think it a bit drastic for me to say not using my creative outlets made this much of a difference because if I were praying faithfully, reading my Bible daily, and going to church regularly, these mood-swings should not happen. Years ago, I would have agreed. However, I was doing all these spiritual things and still the innate desire to create beckoned me to participate. God expects increase from the talents He gives us, even if the sole purpose is to keep us refreshed on a personal level—which in turn automatically makes us better witnesses for the Lord. Think about the man in the Bible who *hid his talent in the earth*. He not only lost his talent, he was tormented (Matthew 25:24–30). I don't want to be tormented because I didn't use the talents God has given me, and I'm sure you don't either. Please, prayerfully consider the importance of using your talents and don't allow the cares of this life to *bury* them.

We Cannot Out-Give God

The subject of priority must be open-ended enough to accommodate what life brings us. There may be seasons when God will require service from us above and beyond that which is normal and there will be no opportunity for creative outlets. Those of us who have experienced refreshing through our artistic expressions must guard our hearts against despising times of augmented service, realizing it's impossible to out-give God. When we willingly sacrifice our time and talents for the work of the Lord, Jesus will make a way for the extended periods of service to subside, allowing time again for creative pursuits. For example, each year our church holds a week long youth camp, which includes morning Bible lessons, evening services, sleeping in tents, and several other activities throughout the day. Volunteers run all this and, not only is it time consuming, it's exhausting. It takes weeks of preparation and there is literally no time for artistic endeavors; unless of course it includes craft projects for the kids or writing and practicing skits. The kids always have a great time, though, and it's worth every minute of giving ourselves for the Lord's service. Then after a few days to recover, things get back to normal and working on a creative project becomes a welcomed retreat.

We need to be very careful though, to avoid getting so used to doing other things—even for God—that we become apathetic toward participating in creative activities and don't make an effort to get back to them. We may not notice the lack immediately because we are using all our energies for a good cause; but in time, we will regret the fact that we let the gifts of God slip away. Like anything, if we don't keep at it, it won't seem as significant as it once was. Those of you who *used to* exercise can relate; remember how much better you felt? Even though the benefits are gone and you long for better health, it takes work to get back into an exercise routine. The same is true with the arts; it requires effort to remain committed and the longer you go without it, the harder it is to recover. If you're one that has set your creative outlet aside, you've probably noticed that even if you're in the mood to do something artistic, you usually don't get around to it. Why is this? Because you've forgotten the simple pleasure and powerful impact once experienced from productive creative actions. Thoughts come, such as, "It would take too much effort to get my supplies out and start something new" or "It's been so long since I played my instrument, I've probably forgotten how" and you talk yourself out of it just that easily. You're not alone in this mindset; several people have described similar scenarios to me. But we all have a responsibility to rid ourselves of negative thinking and then purpose in our hearts to pursue the gifts of God.

Fatigue is another major distraction to making creativity a priority. At the end of a long hard day, all most of us want is to unwind, chill out, and do nothing. This approach is okay in intervals and even needful at times, but when it becomes a way of life, it often suppresses the desire to put our creative energies to work. The secret is learning to let the arts fulfill their purpose instead of feeling as if we're forcing an extra activity into our lives. Adding to this problem, we have become an entertainment-oriented society, making it easy to become a spectator rather than an active participant in the arts. Here again, this is acceptable at times, as long as it doesn't take the place of our creative outlets.

Enjoying the Moment

Have you ever stopped, completely stopped, to look at a beautiful sunset? We've all seen them on our way home from work, or to and from some event and think, "How beautiful," as we continue to our next destination. We hardly ever consider how refreshing it might be to actually stop for a moment and enjoy the view. I'll never forget the night several years ago when I was coming home along a road that lies above our village. From that location, the sunset was the most spectacular sight I'd ever seen. I immediately pulled over and parked my car, where I sat in awe. As I watched the sky before me, I lifted a prayer of thanksgiving to Jesus for the privilege of being right there at that very moment. Colors and cloud formations such as I had never seen before. Then it hit me: for the first time, in I don't know how long, I didn't let the opportunity pass. It typically wasn't in my nature to stop for anything; I was always in a hurry, even when I didn't need to be. As I sat there, an unusual calm came over me and my existence, with all its busyness, collided with the reality of God's omnipresence. A display of His awesome grandeur lay before me, prompting stillness and reflection. Slowly, the sky changed, and so did my thoughts, back to the things I needed to do when I got home. There I was, caught in a moment of time between perfect peace and my hectic schedule. This divergence of emotion beckoned me to evaluate the pace at which I lived. Was it necessary? Were there things I could change that would make my life less stressful? If I can't take time to appreciate the life God has given me, including a brief pause for an amazing sunset, then something's wrong. How about you? Does your busy routine keep you from the simple pleasures that make life special?

Since that experience, my pace has slowed and I'm more mindful of the things and people around me; yet occasionally, precious moments still pass me by. It takes a conscious effort on my part not to allow the busyness to creep back into areas that *should be* off limits, such as time for my family and friends, my health, and my art. I was reminded of this recently on a warm, beautiful evening in early June. Ron and I had just heard our two youngest children play their instruments in the school's spring concert. On the way out to the car, I was not talking about the concert or how well they played; no, I was saying how we needed to get home so I could finish planting the garden. There was still a little daylight left and I wanted to take advantage of it. It was then that Colleen spoke up and said, "Gee Mom, let's just enjoy the moment." A dagger of conviction pierced my soul as her passion for life and understanding of what matters most beckoned me to join in her peace. Here I was, a promoter of the arts, and I couldn't even finish soaking in the achievements of these young musicians before other things distracted me.

Think how many days go by, or years for some, where creative actions suffer neglect because of jobs, deadlines, meetings, and other such things. Everything else takes precedence over creative outlets and the lack of use dulls our senses, while endless activities paralyze any artistic desire that remains.

I would like you to take a moment and make a list of everything you do in a day and keep track of it for a week. You'll be amazed at how much time could be set aside for art by a little rearranging of your schedule. It doesn't have to be large blocks of time or even every day, for that matter; but it should be consistently enough to make a difference. Once creativity becomes a priority in our lives, it will freely flow in and through our thoughts and show up in our actions. It's time we cherish the gifts of God and nurture them.

This matter of priority also plays into our walk with God. Sometimes we get so busy that we don't even realize we didn't spend quality time with Jesus. Creativity is a great blessing and a part of God's plan for our lives; but it should never take the place of, or come before, reading the Bible, prayer, and worship. Our relationship with Jesus must always take top priority. "Commit your works to the LORD, and your thoughts will be established" (Proverbs 16:3). In the long run, we will accomplish more and have a better attitude if we take time to stop and let God guide our decisions. He will reveal to us the things that must be done and also help us recognize the distractions that keep us from His perfect will. When we spend time in His presence and learn to hear His voice, we will go about our day more in tune with what truly matters.

chapter six
effort and balance

Whatever your hand finds to do, do it with your might;
for there is no work or device or knowledge or wisdom
in the grave where you are going. Ecclesiastes 9:10

As discussed in the last chapter, lack of time is a major hindrance to creativity and something that cannot necessarily change simply because we want it to. Effort, on the other hand, revolves around determination and doing what it takes to succeed. Natural ability is one thing, using it is another. It grieves me when I hear people say things like, "I could have gone pro . . ." "I was really good at . . ." "I should have become . . ." However, it never happened. Why? The answer may vary depending upon each situation, but it's often the result of a lack of commitment, especially once the desired goal becomes more *work* than anticipated. Eddie has an amazing talent for writing poetry and while he thinks it would be great to have his work published, he hasn't troubled himself with the details needed to make it happen. Every time he writes a new poem, the dream rekindles for a moment, but then it's several months or even longer before he writes again. His passionate words and descriptive flair will most likely not make it to print because his motivation has not surpassed wishful thinking.

A few years back, Pam participated in a theatrical production in our town. During one of the rehearsals, an idea came to mind and she began a quest to write her very own play. She diligently worked on it for months, but then, one day she became frustrated and quit. Over a year passed without any consideration or desire for completing the project. Frustration is an enemy of creativity because it ensnares our ambition at a place of weakness. Eddie and Pam are not the only ones with a drawer full of poems, plays, stories, and/or buried dreams; all across the land there are people who have started projects, but never finished them. Visions of greatness can only carry us so far; the rest comes down to determination, dedication, and hard work. Recently, Pam purposed anew to overcome what she had previously deemed "a failure" and set out to complete her play. She is now in the process of looking for a publisher.

Innate ability is not enough. We could have all the talent in the world and a good portion of desire, but if we're not consistent in our training and resolute toward seeing a thing through, the result will inevitably fall short of greatness. On the flip side, we could have less natural ability than the next person, but end up with more skill and accomplishments because of a willingness to work, and the determination to push through to completion.

Effort effects outcome. Regardless of what we do, it should be done with unwavering perseverance and the best possible attitude. Colossians 3:23 says, "And whatever you do, do it heartily, as to the Lord and not to men." *Whatever* is an all-inclusive word, leaving no room for halfhearted attempts at anything. When it comes to employment, employers expect work completed in a timely and professional manner. At school, teachers require that students at least make valid attempts. Coaches demand effort, anything short of a hundred and ten percent just won't do. Others can expect, look for, and even demand effort from us, but the most effective and promising results materialize when the drive to succeed comes from within. My son, Stephen, enjoys playing soccer and he put it this way: "The games that feel the best to win and the least painful to lose are ones that you've worked your hardest in; the ones where you gave it your all and left everything on the field." He acknowledges effort as a vital key to victory, but also believes it useful when dealing with defeat. It helps him recognize his weaknesses and makes him more determined to improve for the next game. Effort does not guarantee favorable results, but it certainly helps the persistent.

Though our form of creative expression should be enjoyable and relaxing, it will take a good deal of practice and perseverance to develop our talents to their full potential. We must ask ourselves if we are willing to do what it takes to go beyond our present ability to gain the skills needed to have the most impact. Are we willing to try repeatedly, sketch after sketch, rough draft after rough draft, if need be? When we want something badly enough, it becomes a priority: the process becomes a way of life and the results are usually worth our efforts.

Facing Weaknesses

Our attitude toward life plays an important role in our ability to be who God has created us to be. However, having the right outlook may require changing our vantage point. If the view we have of ourselves is disappointing or mediocre, we are not seeing what God sees in us. This mind-set shows up in our mannerisms and others can easily detect our insecurities. But this is not God's will for our lives, and just as an object cannot conceal its specific shape while the light is on, neither can negative thoughts of ourselves remain once His light shines in our hearts. Psalm 119:130 tells us, "The entrance of Your words gives light; It gives understanding to the simple." Yet, we must act upon God's word if we want a constructive outcome. "Being confident of this very thing, that He who has begun a good work in you will complete it until the day of Jesus Christ" (Philippians 1:6).

Within the vast range of personalities that God created, most of us have the desire to be good at something, especially in the area of talents. When a skill comes naturally to us, it's easier to get involved and improvements evolve quickly. As a result, we have a tendency to work harder at our strengths because they make us feel good about ourselves. There needs to come a point in our lives though, where we willingly work on weaknesses, so God can strengthen and expand His purpose for our lives. For example, you may have an amazing voice and sing beautifully, but if you're shy, the gift will probably go unnoticed because of your fear to stand in front of people. Therefore, God will require you to work on conquering this lack of confidence so He can use your talent.

Most of us have probably heard the expression "all work and no play." This is not what we're looking for; it distorts our view and limits our abilities. To illustrate, we may have a great paying *sedentary* job, but if we do not eat right and never exercise, poor health will ensue, even though we have money in the bank. A healthy balance is the essence of success. Again, we might be really outgoing, yet lack social graces and end up offending people. Colossians 4:6 says, "Let your speech always be with grace, seasoned with salt, that you may know how you ought to answer each one." Cultivating an attitude of grace will make our outgoing personalities flourish and become something God can utilize. As long as our skills, activities, or character traits remain out of kilter, our weaknesses will overpower our strengths.

Another illustration would be that of a basketball player: he may be able to shoot from anywhere on the court with great accuracy, but if he never takes the time to practice foul shots, his percentage from the foul line will most likely be poor. This could cost his team a close game, leaving him with regret for not having mastered his skill by overcoming this weakness. A tennis player can have a powerful serve and a strong forehand return, but if his backhand is weak and inconsistent, he will not excel in competition. To be a complete player he must put effort into the areas of his game that hold him back. Once mastered, look out! Artistic talents are developed in much the same way. If we want to be good at what we do, we must be willing to work at the parts of the process that challenge us.

To master any ability, we must approach the whole concept with the idea of breaking it into attainable parts and then successfully putting it back together. For some time now, I have been fairly good at drawing and shading clothing, but lacked skill when it came to drawing hands and faces. This was a problem because I didn't take the time required to work on hands and faces for them to become easy to me; consequently, the struggle continued. I definitely needed to work on this area, but my weakness extended farther than this—the real root of the problem was that I never wanted to "waste my time practicing." I just wanted to do complete works of art. Until this attitude changed, the images I did of people were always second rate.

Since then I've had the opportunity to do a charcoal portrait of my niece's children and I actually practiced drawing hands and faces before getting started. It was undoubtedly the best portrait I've ever done. It wasn't just better; the children looked alive. My efforts paid off.

Why do we tend to avoid the things we don't do well? There could be several reasons, but I want to focus on one that we often don't take to heart. That is, with a little time and effort, weak spots can be turned into strengths, or at least become stronger. How many of you have noticed that God doesn't let us off the hook so easily when it comes to character flaws? He is faithful to bring about circumstances that make us deal with personal limitations, since He knows it will make us better for His service. We can apply this truth to our talents by confronting our weaknesses with a determination to prevail. In Chapter Twelve, I will discuss how we can use our talents to share the Gospel. This is why it's of utmost importance for us to work at improving every area of our lives and why we should take seriously the need to excel at our creative outlets.

Physically Fit

God created mankind with the ability to operate in three different realms: the physical, the emotional, and the spiritual. All three are necessary and need attention to facilitate health and wholeness. Therefore, I will address each one, starting with the physical. The advantages to eating right and exercise are considerable. All who have the willpower to do so on a regular basis are usually stronger and healthier than those who don't. It takes work and persistence, though.

My sister, Sally, is an avid distance runner, and has even run marathons. She initially took up running to get back in shape and lose the extra weight she gained after a difficult pregnancy. To her surprise, however, she found running also helped relieve stress and energized her emotionally. This is because the benefits of staying physically fit affect the soul. I'm not implying we should all become distance runners, but it is up to each one of us to find and work at a consistent exercise routine, one suited to our individual needs.

There are those who don't diet or exercise until they become overweight, worn-out, and unhappy with themselves. Often, health problems jump-start the necessity for a life-style change. My father-in-law came down with sugar diabetes in his early seventies, but ironically, it was a good thing for him. At his Doctor's instructions, he purposed to change his diet and became very active; which kept the diabetes in check. In addition, when he made these required adjustments, he found his energy returned and a fresh outlook on what was important to him emerged. Getting started on the road to physical health is invaluable, no matter how old you are. Keep in mind, this is only a part of the bigger picture; the spirit and soul need attention too!

Spiritually Fit

Physical health, by itself, cannot make us invincible. Broccoli, carrots, and mangoes, along with consistent exercise, may help us to live longer, stronger lives, but if we haven't surrendered our spirit to the will of God, a void exists and we are not complete. A nourished spirit and a sound mind must coincide with strength of body.

If you are not familiar with the parable of the "Sower and the Seed," it can be found in Mark 4:3–20. Here Jesus tells us about the different kinds of soil the seed fell on and how the seed fared in each situation. He then related it to our spiritual condition. When I read this parable, I usually choose what kind of soil I am and the super-spiritual side of me always picks the "hundred-fold Christian." Then one day, as I read this parable anew, I stopped to evaluate my walk with God and realized that over the years I've acted as different kinds of soil. On occasion, the word of the Lord fell on a hard heart and a deaf ear, like the seed falling by the wayside. This attitude could produce no fruit in my life until I repented. There've been other seasons where the cares of this world consumed my time and crowded out my commitment to prayer. I've even encountered offenses and had to send my roots deep in the Lord or I could have fallen away. Thankfully, for the most part, the soil of my heart has remained soft and pliable, allowing God to bring forth fruit, though it hasn't always been easy. How about you? Have you ever acted or reacted differently to the word of God depending upon what you were going through? Have there been seasons when your commitment wavered? "Therefore, my beloved brethren, be steadfast, immovable, always abounding in the work of the Lord, knowing that your labor is not in vain in the Lord" (1 Corinthians 15:58). Each of us must be personally mindful that it takes endurance and unfailing diligence to stay spiritually strong and productive. Proverbs 4:23 tells us, "Keep your heart with all diligence, for out of it spring the issues of life."

A natural garden needs tending to produce a harvest: the earth tilled and prepared, seeds planted, weeds eliminated, water and cultivation, (all things that require effort on the gardener's part). But then what? If the gardener wants another crop, he/she must re-till the ground, plant new seeds, and start the process over . . . year after year. One harvest could be abundant, but the next crop could fail if not properly cared for. So it is with the spirit within us. I'm sure most of us have had great seasons of harvest in our walks with the Lord, but if we are honest with ourselves, other seasons have not been as fruitful because we neglected some of our responsibilities. If we don't guard our hearts and work at spiritual growth, our root system won't be strong enough for us to stand when trials come. Matthew 5:45 tells us it, "rains on the just and on the unjust." We are not exempt from difficulties just because we've accepted Jesus into our hearts. Trials strengthen us if we remain faithful to tend the soil of our hearts by keeping it soft and fertile to receive the word of the Lord. "And let us not grow weary while doing good, for in due season we shall reap if we do not lose heart" (Galatians 6:9).

It takes a continual pressing "toward the goal for the prize of the upward call of God in Christ Jesus" (Philippians 3:14). Even good ground will only produce thirty-fold if we are not consistent in watering the seeds and cultivating what God plants in our hearts. When spiritually fit, we are secure in our soil, strong in our faith, and able to produce the fruit of a hundred-fold Christian. It's when we get distracted or succumb to spiritual laziness that our soil becomes un-kept, weedy, and dry.

Creatively Fit—The Soul Realm

You've probably heard the expression, "They are so heavenly minded, that they are no earthly good." If our whole purpose were heaven, then God would have made us angels. 3 John 1:2 tells us, "Beloved, I pray that you may prosper in all things and be in health, just as your soul prospers." In this verse, the word *prosper* means: to help on the road, succeed in reaching, to succeed in business affairs. God gave us emotions and put us in a physical world with a supernatural connection. It's His will that we learn how to successfully pull all three together so we can be more productive in this life.

Creative outlets, even if they take physical exertion or have spiritual connotations, primarily affect the soul and help us remain mentally strong. I am aware that creativity is not the only way to keep on top of things emotionally, but it certainly helps when utilized as an exercise routine. By taking creative action, the benefits flow back and forth between the other two realms. When in control of our emotions, it takes less effort to watch our weight and exercise. It's also easier to keep Jesus in the forefront of our thoughts, making us more sensitive to His will.

Those of us who consider exercise beneficial will press through even when we don't feel like it. We that understand that maintaining good works is vital to our spiritual well-being will continue to do so: daily reading God's word, praying, and faithfully attending church. However, some of you reading this may not believe the advantages of creativity are worth the effort required and will put it aside until the mood is right. But the mood will seldom *be right* if commitment wanes. For example, I enjoy painting, but I hate getting started. My willpower has to surpass my apprehension of a blank piece of paper, but once it does, favorable results usually follow.

Creativity challenges our observation and thinking which keeps our minds alert and strong. Yet expanding our brainpower takes exercise just like increasing muscle tone. When I first started writing, one hour was all I could do and then my brain felt tired. In time, however, my mental capacity grew to the place where I could write for several hours at a time and I felt invigorated. Even so, I would like to challenge you to become creatively fit. The benefits will not only give you a boost emotionally and help you feel better; they will also improve your abilities, increase your thinking, sharpen your senses, and ultimately advance your confidence.

Balance Between Effort and Pressure

Pressures not only affect our efforts, they affect our peace, our witness, and our eternal purpose. Because we are created to be creative, our ambitions and attitudes play a role in determining our ability to succeed. Finding the correct line of perspective will help us know when enough is enough and when we've pushed ourselves beyond a healthy balance.

Do you know people who are so goal oriented that they don't have time for family or friends, much less to enjoy a creative outlet? How about people who are creative and very talented, but somewhere along the line life got in the way and they stopped making time for art? There was too much else to do . . . or so they thought. These people don't seem to enjoy life very much. There are the temporary highs, moments of happiness—when success comes—but before long, it's back to the same pattern of striving for more. There are also those who never seem to succeed, even though their determination remains undaunted. Others always climb the ladder ahead of them and they're miserable. What fills the in-betweens is a lot of hard work and stress, but not much satisfaction. Have any of these things happened to you?

1 Timothy 6:6 tells us, "Now godliness with contentment is great gain." Part of our *fallen* nature gravitates toward discontentment and jealousy, distracting us from God's purposes and His peace. Some have even fallen into a pattern of striving for other things to fill the void, but this often leads to needless activity and frustration.

People who are performance oriented often project that onto their children as well. Dan recalled the time when he came face to face with this mind-set after a football game his twelve-year-old son had just played. Troy was the quarterback; he put forth a valiant effort, did an exceptional job, and was quite excited about his performance as the two walked off the field together. His father's assessment? "You played well son, but you could have done better if you would have . . . and . . ." Then out of the corner of his eye, Dan caught sight of the assistant coach who happened to be walking along side of them. He was shaking his head in disappointment. At that moment, Dan realized he expected too much from his son. He couldn't even let Troy enjoy his achievements in today's game before addressing ways he could play better. Dan's desire for flawless precision from his son was unrealistic and didn't encourage the normal growth process. His critical response made Troy wonder if he'd ever be good enough for Dad. Dan came to the realization that allowing Troy to celebrate his present success was crucial to maintaining his love for the game and his desire to improve.

For those of us who are parents, or have influence over the lives of others, we need to be careful not to destroy their willingness to participate because of the demands we put on them to perform. There is a difference between pushing someone with talent and setting unrealistic goals that are beyond their present ability. Pressure builds character. To illustrate, the image in a coin is formed when pressure is applied to push away all that is not part of the desired image. But if the force is too great, the coin is destroyed along with its value. There is nothing wrong with pushing someone to succeed, as long as it's not in excess. The best thing we can do is encourage others to positively work at improving their talents without crushing their desire to do so.

One final thought about effort and finding our worth by the things we achieve: at times, the results will be out of our control. Do you remember what happened at the Pairs Figure Skating Competition during the 2002 Winter Olympic Games? A majority of those who watched the Canadian couple's program thought they should have won the Gold Medal. Clearly the judges' decision to award the gold to another pair of skaters shocked people the world over and greatly disappointed the Canadians—even though their performance reached across cultural bounds and entertained all who watched. They showed amazing athleticism and artistry tied together in a beautiful package of excellence, but it still came short of gold. A few days later, after much public outcry, the couple received co-champion honors and obtained a Gold Medal, but what if that didn't happen? Think about it: if they based their worth on the judges' verdict, it could have destroyed their confidence and ruined their creative future.

This instance proves we cannot always base our worth on someone else's opinion of us. Nor should the amount of effort we put forth revolve solely around results, especially once the outcome extends beyond our control. Sometimes our actions have to carry us despite the assessment of a few, because there *will* be others who appreciate our creative expression, even if we don't have a medal or an award to prove it. In competitions, as well as in life, not everyone can finish on top, but the challenge to get there should make us better. We must not allow circumstances to overwhelm us and cause us to lose sight of God's purpose for doing a thing in the first place.

I would like each of you to take a moment and consider how you handle challenges and pressures. There are those who need a challenge to get motivated, to provoke deeper thought, and gain better results. Pressure, whether internal or external, does not have to be consuming and when handled properly, it can be constructive. How we look at effort and hard work will determine how enjoyable the process will be and will ultimately control how much influence our lives and our actions have on others.

chapter seven

observe with purpose

*And the man said to me, son of man, look with your
eyes and hear with your ears, and fix your mind
on everything I show you . . . Ezekiel 40:4*

Observation is merely the act of seeing and consciously taking notice. Sounds easy, right? Why then is it so hard? I like the explanation I overheard in a quilt shop once. Two women were chatting while they waited for their fabric when, out-of-the-blue, one of them mentioned the unique stitching on the dress of a rag doll propped at the end of the counter. The clerk was pleased and complimented the woman on her keen sense of observation. "Oh yes," she responded with a laugh, "I'm very observant when I'm not distracted." I suspect distraction is the case a good portion of the time. Most of us are either in a hurry and don't bother to look; or we have tunnel vision and only take interest in what seems worthy of our attention. The problem with this approach is that we miss more than we realize. Furthermore, in our world of death and destruction, we often choose not to see, closing our eyes to all that is ugly or uncomfortable. This may seem easier at the time, but in reality, it sears our conscience and limits our ability to observe with purpose. Jeremiah put it this way, "My eyes bring suffering to my soul . . ." (Lamentations 3:51). When we actually *see* what we're looking at, it affects our thoughts and emotions, often causing us to take action.

To hear, smell, feel, and taste are also invaluable, assisting in our overall perception of the world around us. God's design of the human body is incredible, and learning to maximize our sensitivity to the things around us will produce a stronger and more creative output. Psalm 34:8 tells us, "Oh, taste and see that the LORD is good; blessed is the man who trusts in Him!" God not only asks us to see, but also to taste—to partake of His nature, making it an integral part of our lives. Acts 17:27 adds the dimension of feelings, "That they should seek the Lord, if haply they might feel after him, and find him, though he be not far from every one of us" (KJV). Proverbs 1:5 emphasizes hearing, "A wise man will hear and increase learning, and a man of understanding will attain wise counsel." In the Song of Solomon, there are several references to the sense of smell, heightening Solomon's mood. Senses improve our ability to drink in and experience life to the fullest. The more attentive we are to the things around us, the more our senses come into play.

Our observation skills also augment when we take interest in the subject at hand. Once, while sitting with friends in the gymnasium of a neighboring high school, waiting for a basketball game to start, Brian pointed out that the covers to the basket cranks were all upside-down. (These cranks are used to raise the basketball hoops out of the way when not in use.) I was surprised that he noticed them when I saw how near the rafters they were. But then Brian likes working with machinery and the mechanics of them; he observed the upside-down numbers because his interest caused him to look in the direction of the basket cranks.

My mom has an affinity for bird watching. Every time we go somewhere together, she will point out the different birds she sees. We even saw a bald eagle once, which is extremely rare in our part of the country. I would have missed that opportunity had we not been together. She will also draw my attention to picturesque or oddly shaped trees. This may seem simple and insignificant, yet when seen through creative eyes, well worth the look. Now, I'm more apt to watch for birds, interesting trees, old barns, and other such things, which in turn have improved my observation.

The lines and curves of architecture can be captivating as well. Historical eras and cultural differences also give cities a wealth of visual interest along with the people who fill them. No matter where you live or what your interests are, there is always plenty to see. Sometimes it just takes a little effort on our part to have these visual stimulants register into our thought processes, making them useful.

What Catches Your Eye?

Learning to look is only the first step; from here, observation can expand past our initial glance. Several years ago, my oldest daughter, Karen, entered a pencil drawing in the New York State High School Arts Competition, where she received a *Gold Key*. She hadn't anticipated winning an award, because, although her drawing was quite good, she didn't think it was the best in her category. What was it that captured the eyes of the judges over several other strong drawings? Perspective. In this drawing, Karen depicts an unusual angle, one you wouldn't expect to see. Her composition shows the intrigue of a young girl climbing a tree; but what makes it interesting, the girl is looking up at you, as if you were already in the tree, encouraging her to come higher. Her adorable face, with big inquisitive eyes provokes thought. What is she looking for? Has she seen a bird's nest and wants a closer look? Is her kite stuck on the next limb and she's determined to rescue it? Could her favorite place to sit be just a few branches higher? This drawing succeeds, not only because the perspective is artistically correct, but also because it compels those who take the time to look, to reflect upon the young girl's actions. Karen has two forms of perspective working together—one technical, the other speculative, both captivating and essential parts of art.

We cannot observe with purpose unless we pay attention to the things we see. This reminds me of the time I had just finished hanging a new display of artwork in a conference room. One of the business-men arrived early for a meeting and after a brief introduction, our conversation turned to the paintings. Usually there was a greater variety of artwork, but on this particular day, the exhibit consisted mostly of landscapes done in watercolor. One of the few exceptions was a unique colored pencil drawing. When Alex asked me about it, I casually responded, "Yes, this one is kind of weird."

"But that is why my eye was drawn to it," he replied. Just then other guests arrived and the conversation ended. Later that day I asked Alex what it was about the colored pencil drawing that caught his attention.

"At first it was the bright colors and the fact that it was so different from the other paintings." Then after a brief pause he concluded, "It has so much *scope*."

Do you see the progression here? First, Alex was attracted to the drawing because of the visual stimulants of color and diversity. Secondly, he began to ponder the artist's intentions—to *see* with his intellect. In this particular case, the drawing accomplished its purpose because it brought Alex to a place of creative thinking: "It has so much scope." Bright colors initiated his thought process; the subject matter kept the process going.

I challenge you to consider why certain forms of art catch your eye. Do you find them engaging because you're impressed with the art-ist's skill? Does subject matter, such as the dreamy plot of an appealing land or seascape calm your mood? Are you partial to modern art with bright colors and interesting themes? How about photo-realism with great lighting? Our individual tastes will make a difference in what gets our attention. Yet, no matter what we favor, something should catch our eyes, turn our heads, and cause creative thoughts to begin.

Don't stop here, either. Let your appreciation of the arts go beyond personal preferences. Try looking in earnest at what doesn't immediately catch your eye; you may find redeeming qualities in artistic expressions that were of no interest to you before. I know my definition of impressive art was once very limited. I also realize this attitude restricted my ability to be innovative as an artist. I needed to look outside myself with a willingness to find merit in what was "not my style." Over the years, I've grown to enjoy a variety of art and my observation skills have increased, simply by opening my heart as well as my eyes. Yours can, too.

We can increase our artistic appetites by slowing down and taking time to focus. For example, when walking through a gallery or museum, don't just quickly scan the room. Give specific attention to each piece. Think about whether or not it appeals to you and ask yourself, "Why or why not?" Reflect on purpose as well as artistry. Try holding your gaze for a moment longer while looking at art you don't particularly care for and ask yourself if there is anything that could improve your opinion. By the way, the answer does *not* have to be "yes" to every piece, but you may discover you like some styles you didn't think you would, simply by observing with purpose.

I like to make a comparison between art and food. Have you ever given certain foods a second chance and found you liked them? When I was a child, I did not care for peppers and onions. Years later, I gave them another taste and have since enjoyed the added flavor and diversity they bring to a meal. The same has been true with my appreciation of art. In the past, I wouldn't give certain styles an ounce of consideration. Through the years though, I've become more accepting and supportive of a greater variety. I'm not talking about ungodly art, but rather a whole range of art, which now stimulates my reflection beyond an initial glance or response.

I encourage you to take every opportunity to expand your scope through observation. Pay attention to the details that give each piece purpose beyond your first impression and learn to follow patterns of thought that immerge from increased visual awareness. Don't be surprised when you find this process activates the innovative resources within you and enhances your own creative output. I know this works because I've learned to include points of interest to my art, which in turn provoke extra contemplation. Just as peppers and onions add zest to food, so a broader variety of art will add flavor to your individual artistic expression.

Be true to yourself, though, and don't ignore your own personality while viewing art. Realistically—no matter how hard we try, there will always be types and styles of art that won't suit your tastes or mine. Yet, the art we dislike, some people will find meaningful, while still others will find fantastic, and vice versa. This is how we maintain individuality and diversity; otherwise, creativity would become prosaic and lose purpose.

Learning to Pay Attention

Seeing is one thing; paying attention to detail is another. Though many things come daily into our view, very few actually register into the thought process. As you read this next section, think of a situation in your life that makes this example relevant to you.

As a group of landscape artists climbed the rugged terrain of a popular mountain to reach a point of great views and possible paintings, Jeff suddenly stopped and pulled out his sketchpad. "What are you doing?" Trevor inquired, "We haven't reached our destination. Besides, what's so interesting here?"

Not intimidated by Trevor's remark, Jeff answered, "You guys go on ahead; I'll be along in a few minutes."

By the time Jeff rejoined the group, everyone else had found their spot of choice and were working on the layouts for their paintings. Jeff took a good look around and began his second drawing.

Later that afternoon, while the artists took a break, Chloe inquired, "So Jeff, are you going to show us your first sketch?"

"Sure" he said, as he flipped back a few pages. To every ones surprise, perfectly situated amongst the sharp rocks that lined the trail was a single wild flower. No one else in the group had noticed it. Jeff went on to say, "The flower seemed drastically out of place to me; so soft and delicate, yet growing in this rugged and unlikely setting." He hesitated and then concluded, "I was intrigued by the fact that this flower lived in complete isolation, yet it stood strong and uninhibited—to me, a symbol of hope."

Chloe, still absorbed in the drawing, admitted, "I was so focused on reaching our destination, I never thought to look for artistic expression along the way."

Jeff found beauty in a place where the others didn't think to look. He didn't require the perfectly picturesque view that awaited him at the mountaintop because he trained his eye to observe the details of his present location. Consequently, creative ideas are available to him in all situations. He simply chooses to be mindful of his surroundings, looks for something interesting, and takes action by putting his impression of it on paper.

Many artists are stuck believing a masterpiece has to be impressive or grand. Actually, art can communicate powerful thought through just a glimpse of something more, leaving the rest to the onlooker's imagination. What may seem inconsequential, like Jeff's flower amongst the rocks, really has the potential of grandeur, simply by the message it delivers. The other artists with Jeff remained focused on their original goal of painting at the mountaintop, where undoubtedly the view was amazing. Unfortunately, their inflexible resolve caused them to forfeit artistic opportunities along the way.

Things that most of us would walk right past without noticing can become visually stimulating when seen as an art form. If it evokes thoughts not otherwise reflected upon, observation and communication are achieved. The piece succeeds whether considered impressive or not.

Jeff's watchful approach also opens the door to individuality.

When applied to our lives, it allows each one of us to see and respond according to our own personalities. What appeals to one may not even catch the eye of another, or we could all look at the exact same thing and see it differently—because it's not only what we observe, it's how we perceive it. For instance, some never actually focus on what they see; they are oblivious to what's around them. If they saw an automobile accident, they could not give an accurate description of the scene or what had happened. Others choose to focus on details and look intently. They would likely be able to answer most questions concerning the same accident. The rest of us lay somewhere in between these two extremes and each of us would have a different account of what took place. In part, because of the angle at which we saw the accident and partly because of how closely we chose to pay attention. This brings us back to individuality. Just as we are created distinctly unique, likewise no two impressions of a single event, artistic opportunity, or expression will be interpreted exactly the same. Perception varies and is fundamental to translation; as a result, it increases our capacity for diversity and appreciation.

Bias also affects our sight. Consider a sporting event; if an official makes a call in our favor, he saw the play correctly and is competent. Yet if the call went against our team, the official is as blind as a bat and doesn't know anything. Desire for victory obscures our ability to see objectively.

Personal faith also affects our perception. Those who have little or no faith will be more apt to see things in a negative light, while those who are confident in their faith will see with eyes of hope, even in dark situations. John 20:1–12 demonstrates how a number of people can look at the same thing, yet have varying testimonies. Mary Magdalene comes to Peter and John and tells them the sepulcher of Jesus is empty. Immediately they run to the tomb that they might *see* for themselves. John arrived first and looking in saw the linen clothes, but did not go into the sepulcher. When Peter caught up, he boldly ran straight into the cave and saw the linen clothes as well, but he also saw the napkin that was about his head not lying with the linen clothes. A few minutes later, John ventured into the tomb. Looking more closely, he saw and believed Jesus had risen from the dead. After Peter and John returned home, Mary lingered about the tomb weeping. As she wept, she stooped down and looked into the sepulcher. Here she saw two angels in white sitting, the one at the head and the other at the feet, where the body of Jesus had lain.

Notice how all three saw something different. John, at first, looked quickly and from a distance; he didn't see the whole picture. A few minutes later, after taking a good look around and from a better vantage point, not only did how much he saw changed, but his thoughts changed also . . . "he believed." Peter's strong, assertive personality, clearly seen throughout the Gospels, remains true here in observing for himself. He went right in and got a close-up view immediately. Mary lingered and wistfully looked *again*; this time, through eyes of hope, and she saw angels. God brought comfort by allowing her to see into the realm of the spirit. Learning to pay attention is about observing more than natural things. The Spirit of God enlightened Mary's eyes and she became aware of things not normally seen. This kind of sight becomes accessible as faith permeates daily living.

Though we live in a natural world with plenty to see and hear, our perception can go deeper than the surface. For example, by looking earnestly into ones eyes, we can see beyond physical appearance. As we exercise this ability, we can detect a broken heart, a tranquil hope, a secret fear, an amiable personality, a wistful dreamer, etc. During my six-year battle with fibromyalgia, despite the happy face I attempted to wear, my friends could detect the depth of pain because it emanated through my eyes. It was not hidden from those who observed with purpose. Because they chose to look past my facade, they saw my need and brought me comfort.

Past the Beautiful and the Obvious

As our observation improves and we willingly become aware of our surroundings, we will develop a talent for recognizing other types of inconspicuous flowers, such as the overlooked child lost among the rocks and thorns of a deteriorating home life. When accustomed to looking only for superficial beauty, we tend to shy away from the unappealing, which releases us from any costly involvement. On the other hand, learning to seek out and identify those obscure creative possibilities, beyond the beautiful and the obvious, helps sharpen our ability to detect more than art. Looking beneath the surface and allowing life experiences to impact us on a more personal level strengthens our compassion and our ability to make a difference. This is why it's important to develop these skills outside the studio. Practice looking, no matter where you are. You may see an idea for your next project, or better yet, you just might notice someone in need or a situation that requires a solution.

Observation can be a mere acknowledgement of what's going on around us, or a compelling force causing us to take action. The more we observe with purpose and make sense of what we see, the more creative our thoughts become. Ultimately, these thoughts can affect our disposition and influence our direction.

At times, our only action will be a reaction, an emotional response, but no deliberate thought is given to constructively getting something done. Let's consider the homeless for a moment. If you live where you see homeless people every day, you may overlook them because you know there's not a whole lot you can do. These people become a part of the landscape, no longer *consciously* seen, as the eyes, along with the heart, become calloused. We've probably all done this, distancing ourselves from things we don't want to face or assume we cannot change. This way we don't have to deal with consequences that surface from thinking or feeling obligated to get involved. Without conscious sight, there is no significant thought—with no significant thought, there is no conviction—with no conviction, no action seems necessary. We feel safe and justified with this way of handling things.

Now, let's change the scenario a bit. Suppose you live where there are no homeless people and then visit a major city. You will actually be more apt to *see* the homeless, which in turn will provoke thought. Your first thoughts may be of repulsion or pity. However, if you think about it long enough, possible ways of helping may come to mind. I remember my friend, Debbie, telling me about a co-worker who went to NYC on a business trip. While she was there, she saw quite a few homeless people and began to think, "Can I make a difference?" It was near Christmas and every year her place of employment did some kind of charitable outreach. Because of this, she came up with the idea of asking everyone that was willing to donate a new blanket for the homeless. Several blankets were collected, sent to a NYC mission, and distributed to those in need. Observation, in this case, caused the thought process to begin, which ultimately inspired a creative action. These blankets did not put a roof over anyone's head, but they did help keep some people a little warmer that winter.

Proverbs 22:9 tells us, "He who has a generous eye will be blessed, for he gives of his bread to the poor." This has to do with how we see people and our willingness to look on others with favor, to reach out and meet their needs. One of the best ways to improve observation skills is to look past our personal comfort zone and notice those around us. Once we do this, we can move a step further and ask God to give us a generous eye. We will never see every situation, nor can we necessarily do anything more than pray. Nevertheless, when we are sensitive to the needs of others, God can burden our hearts with certain ones and supply us with a creative word of encouragement or the means to help.

The parable of the sower, found in Matthew 13, tells us that some seeds fell on stony ground, fought briefly for life, but had no place to send down their roots. Over time, the plants withered and died. Do we notice those struggling individuals who are stuck in a hard place? Let's not condemn them unawares. We have power to breathe supernatural life into people's circumstances by asking God to transplant their weary souls by rivers of living water. A helping hand can also inspire real hope, especially when extended from the heart, because someone took the time to look deeper than the surface.

If we only look for beauty in high places, many a lonely traveler gets overlooked; just like the wild flower that only caught the eye of one. Is your observation programmed to only respond to the grandiose? Is your sight limited to visible beauty? If your answer is yes, notice how your eye quickly moves elsewhere when something is unappealing. Be assured, it takes effort to develop skills for discovering beauty in unexpected places, especially if this beauty is not evident to the natural eye. Our prayer should be, "Lord, help me to look with my eyes, hear with my ears, and set my heart upon all that You want me to see. Create in me a thoughtful attentiveness, willing to take action, and the ability to use the gifts You have given me for the greater good." Learn to observe with purpose!

chapter eight
think and act with purpose

*Finally, brethren, whatever things are true, whatever things
are noble, whatever things are just, whatever things are
pure, whatever things are lovely, whatever things are of
good report, if there is any virtue and if there is anything
praiseworthy—meditate on these things. Philippians 4:8*

As the day dawns, we arise with an array of thoughts pertaining to
who we are and what we have to accomplish. Every single day we have
the privilege of choosing the level of impact those thoughts will have;
they are simply another part of the creative journey.

Freedom of thought does not depend upon visual stimulants, although they often jump-start the process. Having studied the paintings of Andrew Wyeth, I find them intriguing because they prompt
questions such as, "What could be on the other side of that door?"
"Where does this road lead?" "Why is that face so sad?" or "What is
the woman thinking?" Wyeth had an uncanny ability to compel those

who observe his art to think past the obvious. His layouts, lighting, and facial expressions all help tell a story without words. What I find most appealing is that the narrative depends totally upon us and can reach as far as we allow our imaginations to carry us.

We've all had projects at school or work that required fresh ideas or new ways of doing things. Usually we begin with familiarities, things previously done; but then our thoughts must delve into untapped resources where possibilities can flourish. The more we challenge our intellectual and creative capacity, the more productive we become.

During one of Cindy's college writing classes, thirty-six different clay pots were set out on a table and the assignment was to give each pot an emotion. Cindy found it easy to categorize the first eight or ten, but then drew a blank; so did the other students. Upon inquiry, the Professor explained the purpose for this exercise was to make them think past initial responses, to move beyond quick, obvious emotions, and to release thoughts and feelings concealed by lack of use. He explained how the depth of thought could increase through necessity, augmenting vocabulary as well as experience.

We often stop thinking at the obvious because it's easier and requires no extra time or energy. As with prayer and meditation, creative thinking takes effort to become an active part of life. The more we do it, the easier it becomes. Psalm 92:5 tells us, "O LORD, how great are Your works! Your thoughts are very deep." When we allow the Spirit of God to permeate our thoughts, He provides strength and ability to think beyond the norm. Moreover, the amount of consideration given to something will make a difference in how much we participate. For instance, I have a tendency to procrastinate; if I think the rationale for getting something done in advance is sufficient, I'll gladly do it. However, if my thoughts aren't convincing, what I have to do will remain until the last possible opportunity. Therefore, how I interpret my thoughts rules over what I think and I act accordingly. You yourself may procrastinate and think, "What's the big deal as long as things get done?" If you work well under pressure, it may not be a problem.

However, if I wait until the last minute, there's usually a lot more stress involved and, even if the results are favorable, my manners can be far from pleasant. I've learned accurate thinking, with appropriate and timely actions help the overall outcome.

Thinking through Our Beliefs

Many things shape the development of what we think and why we act the way we do, including things our parents, churches, and schools have taught us. There are also life experiences that affect our thoughts, as well as our responses: what we've seen and heard, how we've been treated, and our emotional interactions with others, etc. For example, if someone who has experienced physical abuse views art depicting domestic violence, it will induce a more serious contemplation than it will in someone who cannot relate. A song of worship will ignite passionate expression in those having a personal relationship with Jesus, where individuals who do not know Him lack such zeal, and so forth.

We can train our minds to think and act with purpose, or we can merely *react* to our senses, causing all useful thought to end in a state of languor. We cannot solely revolve our lives around visual and physical stimulants; there must be a strong belief system wherewith we measure our thoughts before taking action. Accepting Jesus into our lives is a start, but by itself is not enough. We must know what we believe, put our faith into practice, and have a tangible hope that is recognizable to all. 1 Peter 3:15 puts it this way, " . . . and always be ready to give a defense to everyone who asks you a reason for the hope that is in you, with meekness and fear." It's more than Sunday religion; it's daily living out our salvation. When we filter our thoughts through the word of God, He'll show us how to communicate the significance of the cross by how we live and through our creative outlets.

This does not, however, completely protect us from having thoughts or feelings that are not of God. Because of our fallen condition, we live within the sphere of right and wrong thinking. It's up to us to maintain healthy patterns of thought, taking into consideration that most of our actions stem from what we believe and how we think. To illustrate, if you believe lying is wrong, contemplating ways to lie and then evade the consequence is unacceptable. Instead, you will think of how to maintain your integrity in the situation according to God's word, even if this means having to admit your fault or deceit. Again, if you consider gossip inappropriate, when someone speaks unkind words about another, you will pursue ways of turning a negative conversation to a positive one; but if not *mindful*, you may well join in the gossip and spread unnecessary pain. 2 Corinthians 10:5 commands that we bring "every thought into captivity to the obedience of Christ." Preserving godly ideals takes effort, which involves going beyond personal gain or acting impulsively.

Experience plays a role in shaping our personalities, but our faith and values should define who we are. Let's imagine for a moment that we've never been hurt by anyone; we think having friends is great and there's no fear of others causing us pain. We don't understand why people can't get along or why some are so bitter. But then an unforeseen schism comes our way and a good friendship is lost—now what do we think? The first thought is usually one of disbelief. Hurt feelings and resentment become a part of the equation, which prepares a place for bitterness to take root. Then God shows up and reminds us of His word, "And be kind to one another, tenderhearted, forgiving one another, even as God in Christ forgave you" (Ephesians 4:32). Now the choice is ours—to obey God's word, or to allow our thinking to persist at the obvious by dwelling on the present heartache. Our actions affect the possibility of reconciliation, shape future relationships, and most importantly, determine our usefulness to God. No matter what the difficulty, if we handle it according to the scriptures, our convictions will control our thinking, allowing them to work together for our good.

Because art is a part of whom we are and not just something we do, it emanates from our personalities. As long as everything's going great, our art will contain a happy, feel-good impression. Nevertheless, if we are in a season of pain, frustration, bitterness, or betrayal—hurt or disappointment can show up in the things we create. Most graffiti, for example, represents negative emotions, even though some of the drawings contain impressive artistic qualities. Graffiti has become a way to vent through the arts; but venting is only good when we can cast our cares upon the Lord and find freedom from harmful sentiments and insubordinate actions. If heart attitudes don't improve by letting go of hurts and trusting Jesus to help us through, they simply become worse, creating a lifestyle of discontentment and retaliation.

Perspective is more than a way to view two-dimensional objects; it's how we see or perceive life and, in most cases, what we feel about our existence will show through our artwork. Consider the paintings of Vincent Van Gogh. In his early twenties, he dedicated his life to the Lord and wanted to preach the gospel, but he was a boring and unskilled orator. He also met with disapproval from church leaders because he gave of his substance to help the poor. Ironic, isn't it? By the course of his actions, he lost his post in the church and had no job. At this point in his life, he began to paint the Dutch peasants and miners, as his heart broke over their impoverished conditions. He himself ended up in grave poverty. Poor and in need, everything changed: his location (he moved from the Netherlands to Paris), his friends, and his outlook. Overwhelmed by these transitions, he went mad and his paintings drastically changed to reflect the crazed behavior that became his artistic trademark for fame. Van Gough suffered with mental illness and finally committed suicide in 1890 at the age of thirty-seven. As his perspective toward life became distorted through circumstance, so did his art.

Hereby we recognize that perspective deals just as much with *how* we look at what we want to create and *why* we want to create it, as it does with the art itself. Thinking how to make art unique takes an ability to portray something internally as well as externally, mixing what we actually see with our personal interpretation and rendering. Writing and music hold their own ability to reflect the author's or musician's take on life as much as individual style. Van Gogh ended his life in a state of perplexed depression. Though his art is unique, interesting, and colorful, his legacy is one of confusion and despair because we cannot separate the art from the artist. This is why it's of utmost importance that we keep our hearts pure and that we maintain our ability to convey a message of hope through the things we produce, even while going through tough situations. Life may attempt to wear us down and cause us to turn from our faith, but in Psalm 27:13 David warns, "I would have lost heart, unless I had believed that I would see the goodness of the LORD in the land of the living." It's all in our perspective.

I challenge you to consider the capacity and depth of your thoughts. Has life thrown you some curves and weakened your resolve? Do you let others do most of your serious thinking for you? If you are one that believes life has no worth or purpose, your thinking will reflect your lack of motivation. However, if you believe life holds great value, no matter what your situation, your mind (and your heart) will continually consider ways to improve things and make life more meaningful. In the early 1800's, slaves nurtured hope by using their imaginations to help them survive hardships and abuse. They found comfort knowing better days were ahead of them. We know not whether their thoughts of heaven were accurate, but their songs of mansions on hilltops in the sweet by-and-by helped to sustain them. Victor E. Frankl, a Jewish man who lived through the holocaust and author of *Man's Search for Meaning*, wrote this: "What alone remains is 'the last of human freedoms'—the ability to 'choose one's attitude in a given set of circumstances.'" If the slaves could *sing* and Frankl could *write* through the depravity of their conditions, it is possible for each of us to overcome any circumstance by choosing to turn our thoughts toward a higher purpose. Our deeds, a product of contemplation and conviction, will determine the level of influence our lives can have on others.

Yet at the same time, we shouldn't need hardships to cause us to think and act creatively. For example, when one believes in educating children, thought evokes ways of making learning easier, and more enjoyable. Colors and visual stimulants grab the children's attention, musical tunes add interest to nursery rhymes and the alphabet, making them easier to remember, and objects are used to simplify math. These things and many more encourage the development of mental growth, all because people thought of ways to use their innate creative ability for the greater good.

Thought Sparked through Action

Have you ever felt dormant or like your creative energies were a bit dull and unproductive? Has it been weeks, or even longer, since you've had a creative thought worth developing? There will be times when innovative ideas are plentiful and taking action seems effortless, but other times scarcer than you could imagine or want to admit. When this happens, it's important to find ways to jump-start the process. Going to museums, galleries, concerts, or plays can do wonders for creative thought. If these things aren't available, try flipping through art books or magazines. Playing inspirational music is a good motivator, and talking with others about their creative pursuits is beneficial as well. Another great place to find inspiration is from your pastor's sermons. When the message is taken to heart, it can influence your art.

Here are a few hands-on ideas to help get those creative juices flowing again. Take a piece of watercolor paper or canvas and randomly splash colorful paint on it with no specific goal in mind. This uncontrolled and spontaneous action is fun, adventurous, and liberating. Watch how you naturally respond to the flow of colors and how ideas arise. You may even see a shape or a color pattern that has the possibility of developing into a successful piece of art. It doesn't matter if the painting works or not because, if for no other reason, it gives you the opportunity to experiment with the paint and an opportunity to think about what transpired as the colors evolved. Keep in mind, it doesn't always have to be about talent. Sometimes it's advantageous to simply see and learn how to incorporate visuals into your thoughts.

Those of you who quilt can do the same thing with scraps of cloth left over from other quilts. Don't feel like you must stay locked into a traditional pattern; it's fun to let the pieces fall and see where your imagination takes you. This exercise also works well with scrapbooking and card making projects.

Musicians, maybe you're locked into one kind of music. Try different styles or melodies; listen for a sound that reflects your mood at that moment and work with it. You may not have a pre-determined plan; but your skills will remain sharp as a result. And who knows, you just might come up with an award-winning tune.

Expressing yourself in a way that is different from what you normally do can be energizing. Whether anything actually comes from your experimentation or if it simply becomes a practice session, your observation, thinking, and artistry were stimulated and kept active by innovative use.

The Importance of Taking Action

Have you ever experienced a wave of enthusiasm toward a creative outlet because of someone else's ability? I have. Whenever I hear an accomplished saxophone player, I feel inspired and think of how wonderful it would be to play with such skill. I dream of greatness, but dreams contain no substance and, as motivational as they may seem, without action, these moments pass and are gone. My saxophone remains in its case, cold and untouched.

If we don't put action to our creative desires, they will dissipate and lose their appeal. Productive thoughts and ideas hold little value if no constructive activity occurs. Had Thomas Edison not applied action to his concept of the electric light bulb, we would still be in the dark. Furthermore, it took an enormous amount of perseverance to view the ideas that didn't work as stepping-stones to get to the one that finally did. We have all gained by his efforts as well as from thousands of other inventors. Then there's Robert Louis Stevenson, who was often confined to his bed because of health problems. But instead of wallowing in self-pity, he wrote poetry and adventure novels. His thoughts carried him to places he could not physically go and gave him a life he could not possess in the natural. Writing kept him emotionally strong and now we enjoy his books because he chose to share his creative outlet with us. Whether they are inventors, writers, poets, sculptors, musicians, or artists, those who succeeded acted upon their thoughts with purpose.

I can relate because there came a time in my life when thoughts concerning creative principles went beyond the layout for my next painting. Yet, lacking action, these concepts helped no one. That is when I decided to write a book. Many ideas ran through my mind, such as its purpose, the way I should do the layout, and even the examples I would use. The notion that I could encourage others to be creative was invigorating and I couldn't wait to get started—right after I finished what I was doing . . . The problem? I never had or took the time to write and years passed. When I finally did get around to it, my thoughts never seemed as lucid as my initial reflection. Therefore, I learned to seize the moment by keeping a notebook with me; this way I was able to secure ideas as they came. Not every whim was worth recording, but I did take action and now I'm a published author—you being the benefactor.

Have you ever thought big thoughts or dreamed big dreams, but never brought them to fruition? Sometimes it takes setting goals to birth the process and a worthy purpose to see a project through to completion.

The Parable of the Talents

If you're not familiar with the parable of the talents, found in Matthew 25:14–30, please take a few minutes to read it. What was your first impression? Did you think God merely wanted results and blessed those who had them? If so, consider this. God was looking for *action*, a faithful implementation of the gifts He had freely bestowed. The two men who labored with their talents prospered because of their efforts. The third man had no increase because he never worked toward developing his talent; but God expected effort from him, just as He did from the men who were given more.

Verse 15 tells us each man received talents according to his own ability—or individual potential. Our abilities are personal and not to be compared with others. God expects us to participate even if our talents seem small or insignificant. Neither should we concern ourselves about whether it's fair if others have more talents. "But indeed, O man, who are you to reply against God? Will the thing formed say to him who formed it, 'Why have you made me like this?'" (Romans 9:20).

Then came the defense from the man with one talent: he said he was afraid (vs.25). He thought fear would justify his lack of action and get him off the hook, "But his lord answered and said to him, you wicked and lazy servant, you knew that I reap where I have not sown, and gather where I have not scattered seed" (vs.26). In reality, he was lazy. He could have also used the excuse that by receiving only one talent, it added to his poor self-esteem issues, but the root of the problem was an incorrect understanding of God's will for his life. God created each of us for a specific purpose and gave us gifts accordingly. We must always remember we are not acting alone—His Spirit dwells within us. "For to everyone who has, more will be given, and he will have abundance; but from him who does not have, even what he has will be taken away" (vs.29). This was the sad conclusion for the man who did not use his talent. John 15:2 tells us, "Every branch in Me that does not bear fruit He takes away; and every branch that bears fruit He prunes, that it may bear more fruit."

Matthew 25:30 tells us the unprofitable servant was cast into outer darkness. He was not productive because he failed to recognize God as the one who gave the talent. Nor did he understand that if he would obey and take action, God would be faithful to bring the increase. Non-involvement with God's ordained purpose for our lives results in anguish. I do not want to be one who joins the unfaithful servant in a place of torment for the lack of trying.

God never asks us to do anything that He hasn't already given us the ability to do and yet, He has not guaranteed an easy journey. "Therefore, my beloved brethren, be steadfast, immovable, always abounding in the work of the Lord, knowing that your labor is not in vain in the Lord" (1 Corinthians 15:58). It will take time and effort to achieve His will. "But He said, more than that, blessed are those who hear the word of God and keep it" (Luke 11:28)! We cannot out-give God.

The process of being creative is just as important as the outcome. We are accountable for our actions and a faithful use of our talents; God is responsible for all increase. This reminds me of Genesis 26, where God told Isaac to stay in a land that was experiencing famine. Verse 12 tells us, "Then Isaac sowed in that land, and reaped in the same year a hundredfold; and the LORD blessed him." There would have been no crop if Isaac had looked at the improbability of increase and decided not to plant. Ecclesiastes 11:4 shows what happens when we rely on natural instincts, "He who observes the wind will not sow, and he who regards the clouds will not reap." Yet verse 6 goes on to say, "In the morning sow your seed, and in the evening do not withhold your hand; for you do not know which will prosper, either this or that, or whether both alike will be good." Isaac chose to walk by faith, as we see by his example. The result? God's favor and provision.

One final thought: our actions go hand in hand with our heart attitude. We can use our talents to bring forth impressive results, but if our goal is only for show or monetary gain, it will not move the heart of God. However, when pure creativity flows out of a heart of love and obedience, God can use our talents for His glory. "For God is not unjust to forget your work and labor of love which you have shown toward His name, in that you have ministered to the saints, and do minister" (Hebrews 6:10).

The next section of this book puts purpose into perspective. Creativity requires thoughts and actions that go beyond us. It's a matter of understanding and activating God's purpose through the arts to advance His Kingdom here on earth. If we dedicate our talents to God's service and work with what we have, He not only promises results, He promises to bring increase from our labors.

section three

principles in action

making memories

chapter nine
matters of the heart

As each one has received a gift, minister it to one another, as good stewards of the manifold grace of God. If anyone speaks, let him speak as the oracles of God. If anyone ministers, let him do it as with the ability which God supplies, that in all things God may be glorified through Jesus Christ, to whom belong the glory and the dominion forever and ever. Amen. 1 Peter 4:10–11

Enthusiasm is necessary when it comes to using and developing talents, but our *motives* also come into play. We should desire God's presence more than His blessings and the Gift-giver more than His gifts. Putting Jesus first and growing in our relationship with Him will increase our sensitivity and availability to minister to others. This is the focal point of Section Three.

Creative expression can change like the wind—the purpose, the method, the mood, and even the results. The difference will depend upon what we are going through at the time, or by what we want to accomplish. That's why we should search our hearts, every now and again, to make sure our motives are still pure. There is nothing wrong with recognition or popularity, but if we are not careful, these things can divert our focus, and open ways for pride to creep in. God desires to use our talents and is pleased when our efforts prosper—except when we allow our abilities to take preeminence over Him.

Connie has a fantastic voice and loves singing for the Lord. There came a time though, when she felt compelled to lay her gift aside. She didn't know for how long, but her desire was to obey the leading of God's Spirit. Motivational issues seemed the probable cause, since Connie lacked confidence. Consequently, she found her self-esteem in the approval of others through her ability to sing well. Nevertheless, Jesus wanted Connie to find her worth in Him, so that when she sang, it would bring glory to her Maker and minister life to those who listened. She sought counsel from her Pastor concerning the situation and together they agreed it would be advantageous to lay her gift aside for a season.

At first, Connie didn't sing at all, not even in the privacy of her own home. However, it wasn't long before discouragement lingered to the point of mild depression. Praying about this, she realized there was nothing wrong with singing and lifting her voice to God. Singing wasn't the issue, the need for an audience was. A year passed before she began accepting invitations to sing again, but this experience brought personal growth, along with a pure heart of worship.

Our Christian walk has a lot to do with matters of the heart, which in turn, affect our creative outlets. Jeremiah 17:10 tells us, "I, the LORD, search the heart, I test the mind, even to give every man according to his ways, according to the fruit of his doings." When our artistic expression pleases the Lord, He will bring increase. But when we make it about us and what we can gain, we limit our effectiveness on an eternal scale, even if we find *success* in this life.

For by grace you have been saved through faith, and that not

*of yourselves; it is the gift of God, not of works, lest anyone
should boast. For we are His workmanship, created in Christ
Jesus for good works, which God prepared beforehand that we
should walk in them. (Ephesians 2:8–10)*

We see by these verses that God expects works, but they must be
done in a godly manner and with a right heart attitude. David cried
out in Psalm 139:23–24, "Search me, O God, and know my heart; try
me, and know my anxieties; and see if there is any wicked way in me,
and lead me in the way everlasting." This is a prayer that we should
pray often, that we might serve the Lord to the best of our abilities.

The Importance of Friends

It's good to have friends with whom we can discuss topics deeper
than the weather, where challenging thought patterns occur, and opinions freely flow. Ideas or methods are taken into consideration that
wouldn't have been otherwise. Creative thinking is a powerful tool,
but it can become dull if sheltered. Close companions help us see
things from a different point of view. Even when in agreement, the
angle can be different enough to bring our attention to something we
may not have seen or thought of before. Friendships like this strength-
en our abilities without threatening our individuality.

One important element in developing effective friendships is
having common interests and, though not all our friends will consider
themselves creative, it definitely helps to have some who understand
our artistic endeavors. I know when I first expressed a desire to write
a book, not everyone was enthusiastic or even encouraging, for that
matter. Most weren't negative, it was more a "good for you" response
and then the subject was changed. Others were gracious and asked of
the subject matter, though doubt was evident in their tone and it was
obvious they never expected it to happen. Because it took years to
finish, I got the, "Oh, you're still doing that?" remarks. Yet through it
all, my close friends faithfully supported my quest. They asked often
of my progress, gladly listened to my latest ideas, and gave me objec-

tive feedback of their own. I found their encouragement refreshing when the end seemed out of sight and now they gladly rejoice in my success.

Our attitudes often reflect the mindset of the area wherein we were raised. I grew up in a rural area where a poverty mentality was prevalent and it seemed easier to stay small and sheltered than it did to promote hope and prosperity. Attempting to break free from this way of thinking is often met with opposition and not everyone rejoices when someone else gets ahead. This outlook flows into the area of talents as well, making it hard to believe *any good could come from an impoverished area.* Then many of you have grown up in large cities and may feel small and insignificant because of the sheer multitude of people. Recognition seems impossible, especially when so many others are striving to be seen and there are those who don't care who they hurt to get ahead. In general, no matter where we live, people often find it easier to "weep with us when we weep," than they do to "rejoice with us when we rejoice." Do they feel slighted? Are they jealous? Part of our fallen nature has a tendency to look out for *me and mine,* causing selfishness to take preeminence over freely giving a deserved compliment.

Nevertheless, when we are willing to encourage, and even push others to be productive, we all benefit in the end! Hebrews 10:24 exhorts, "And let us consider one another in order to stir up love and good works." This positive approach boosts morale and constructive encouragement draws the best out of people. "Therefore let us pursue the things which make for peace and the things by which one may edify another" (Romans 14:19). When possible, surround yourself with people who want to see you and your talents prosper. Search your own heart as well. Are you one that willingly supports others, even when their success could make you feel inferior? The achievements of others should not threaten our confidence or the bond between us. For example, my sister, Suzanne, took up painting only a few years ago and she has already surpassed my artistic skill. She did the painting at the beginning of this section and is well on her way to becoming a known artist. Her increased ability does not lessen mine. Instead, it motivates me to paint, causing me to become a better artist through her enthusiasm and success.

Another matter of the heart concerning friendship and art is that we are usually willing to take advice and even correction, if need be, from those we know sincerely care about us. Seeking the genuine opinions of friends and close colleagues will contribute to productive growth. If you are the one giving suggestions, do it in such a way that it's not condescending or making you look better, smarter, or more talented. I know people who always preface every comment with a comparison about themselves, which usually is not necessary and the remarks often come across as arrogant. Romans 12:10 tells us, "Be kindly affectionate to one another with brotherly love, in honor giving preference to one another." I have friends who like to get my thoughts on their latest piece of artwork and though on occasion I might not tell them what they want to hear, I try to offer my comments in such a way that they know I have *their* best interest and success in mind. I like getting advice in return and my art is better for the asking. I enjoy our friendly critiques because we challenge each other to be the best we can be and we rejoice in each other's accomplishments. "Pleasant words are like a honeycomb, sweetness to the soul and health to the bones" (Proverbs 16:24). So, whether we are the motivator or the motivated, we must make sure that all recommendations are given and received with a pure heart and godly manners.

Valuable interaction stems from being familiar with the temperaments of our friends. When we are sensitive to their needs, we will know when it's appropriate to draw out creative energy by encouragement. We will also discern whether a challenge or spirited goading might be more beneficial. Proverbs 27:17 tells us, "As iron sharpens iron, so a man sharpens the countenance of his friend." The right kind of participation, given at the right time, will do that—making both art and friendship stronger.

There will be seasons when the creative well runs dry and we need help priming the pump! Friends are faithful to support, offer ideas, and pray for us to find fresh inspiration. Ecclesiastes 4:9–10 declares, "Two are better than one, because they have a good reward for their labor. For if they fall, one will lift up his companion. But woe to him who is alone when he falls, for he has no one to help him up." Unfortunately, creative pitfalls are more common than most people realize or want to admit. (I will discuss Hindrances to Creativity in Section Four.) But if we surround ourselves with people that draw the best out of us, we will experience drought less often. Plus, when difficulties do trip us, we won't stay down as long because the helping hand of a friend is ready to assist. Let's encourage one another to keep our creative outlets active and not allow circumstances to shipwreck the process.

The amount of effort we exert toward artistic endeavors will take precedence in determining the level of our success. However, our creative longevity depends in part upon the growth and influence of others, especially from those who are close and can speak into our lives. Our abilities will not have the full impact we are looking for if our focus is only about us and personal preferences. We need both internal and external input. Though what we produce will reflect our unique personalities, at times we must be willing to look outside ourselves for substance, inspiration, and purpose. It may be easier to discuss creative subjects with other artists, but even our *non-artistic* friends can move us to action if we listen attentively and learn to glean ideas from the conversations of life. By looking outward, we are not avoiding our own creative ability, we are adding to it.

Do all our friends have to be creative in the same way as we are? Absolutely not! Our form of art might not even interest some of them, but interaction with a diverse range of people will open doors of opportunity that were closed to us when on our own. Once we begin to see and think creatively, we'll be amazed at what sparks the creative process. A variety of friends is one great way.

Capture the Moment, Make a Memory

Have you ever noticed how many pictures we take while on vacations or at important events such as birthdays, graduations, and weddings? Why is this? Partly because we enjoy showing family and friends who weren't present, but more importantly, they strengthen our memories. Most of us relive precious moments as we flip through photo albums. For some, the memory holds more charm than the event itself, recalling only the good or wonderful things that happened.

This reminds me of the time when Christine told me about a painting she had done on location. As she was putting her things away, a young couple walked by and stopped to look at her work. Then with great enthusiasm, they began to implore Christine to sell the painting to them. She seemed surprised by this request, because, though she had done other kinds of art, this was her first attempt at oil painting and she had not planned to sell it. Then the couple went on to tell their story of how they were married at that very spot and how Christine had captured the beauty of the day, the mood, the water . . . memories came rushing in. The more they talked about it, the more they fell in love with the painting and had to have it! The painting was more than art to this young couple, it was reminiscent of their special day and captured what the photographer could not. Though the newlyweds were not in the painting, it reminded them of their love for each other.

Christine, moved by the couple's passion, agreed to sell. The painting only communicates part of their story, but when conversation turns to it, their guests enjoy hearing the rest. "This is where we had our wedding and the artist did a wonderful impression of the location . . ." For Christine, it was simply a matter of honing her skills, but for the new owners, it captured their hearts and added to an already precious memory.

Over the years, I've done several different paintings for family members. What was the subject matter? Usually a memory. Each piece of art reminded them fondly of a particular person, place, or event. The most memorable request was a primitive style painting of the family farm where my husband and his eight siblings grew up. Using artistic license, I added different seasons, making it easy to reminisce—lilac and rose bushes in bloom, pear and apple trees bearing fruit, and the other trees showing off their brilliant fall colors. Other elements were added as well, such as cows grazing in the meadow and the old-fashioned hay loader, which conveyed the passing of time. The barns and milk house were included and even the sugar shanty stood stoutly, reflecting the many seasons spent making maple syrup . . . all memories. The days of farming are long past and the farm has since been sold, but this artistic rendering aids in preserving the memory of their homestead with all its rustic charm.

More than photos and art can enhance our memories. Poems and songs are often written in light of a present mood or circumstance, yet they offer fresh sentiment upon their recital even years later. Hand-made quilts or crocheted blankets hold more than warmth, the special occasions for which they were fashioned gives them meaning far beyond their particular function. Many of us buy memorabilia at sporting events or while on vacation because we want things to help us remember the special moments in our lives.

Taking this point a step further, it works to our advantage to capture important events and to secure ways of remembering our past. Proverbs 22:28 declares, "Do not remove the ancient landmark which your fathers have set." Our godly heritage lives on, in part, because of the written, visual, and musical history of those who have gone before us. "I will remember the works of the LORD; surely I will remember Your wonders of old" (Psalm 77:11). When we forget our past, or don't record it properly, we begin to lose sight of our purpose and stop fighting for what we believe. It is very important that we learn about our true Christian American History and the men and women that made this country great. Many of them sacrificed all they had for a cause bigger than themselves and for a nation whose blessings they would never share. Understanding our godly heritage brings strength to our values and it encourages us to stand up for what is right. We can do this by promoting what is good.

Reminiscing is good for the soul. It is also good for creative thought, which motivates creative action. When we consider the influence and importance of the arts in society, it is vital that we help to protect the purity of our part in the development and record of history. I challenge you to make your mark count by using the talents God has given you.

chapter ten

creativity and godly boundaries

For we are His workmanship, created in Christ Jesus
for good works, which God prepared beforehand
that we should walk in them. Ephesians 2:10

What is the first thing that comes to mind when you think of boundaries? I think of borders, limits, and restrictions. However, within these parameters, there is also purpose, protection, and enjoyment. Now that we understand a creative future is possible for each one of us, we will turn our attention to laying a wholesome foundation for our artistic expression. The Bible provides a clear outline of how to live and promises blessings for those who follow. It is also encouraging to know that God doesn't just give commands, He leads by example. One of these examples shows up in the first chapter of Genesis. Do you know what God did at the end of each day of creation? He looked at what he had made "and God saw that it was good" (Genesis 1:4,10,12,18,21,25,31). Everything about creation was good, from its quality to its purpose—including the fact that it was *good* as in *not evil!* Here we find the boundary of purity; something we must always respect when using our talents. Beyond that, go for it and let your personality shine through your creative outlet.

Rivers have banks, but from time to time, they overflow. Destruction follows if the excess is too much, but otherwise the soil becomes quite fertile. Good can come from daring to step outside the self-made boundaries of our pre-determined creative limits. Some of history's most famous artists dared to "color outside the lines" so to speak, and brightened our world. Yes, God requires our creative outlets to be *good,* filled with integrity; but He also allows for boldness to expand our talents in innovative and productive ways.

Artistic rules and theories are valuable for a strong foundation; however, sometimes they hinder creative expression. You might find it helpful to practice methods different from your personality. Even if the exercises push you outside your comfort zone, when you return to what's familiar, you will still feel more daring and expressive. Kayla is a perfectionist who finds pleasure in painting detail; yet she recently felt the need to enhance her skills and extend her horizons. Thus, she came to my watercolor class looking for help. For six weeks she did nothing but loose, wet on wet paintings. Now she mixes these lax techniques with the detail she enjoys and has produced a style that suits her well. Kayla was willing to step outside her self-made boundaries and experiment with the paint; in so doing, she conquered personal limitations along with increasing her creative abilities.

A Sure Foundation

Our goal should be to increase in creative skills and the means whereby we impart life and wholeness through the arts. "Who is wise and understanding among you? Let him show by good conduct that his works are done in the meekness of wisdom" (James 3:13). We won't consistently create that which is good unless our foundation is built upon God's word and His Spirit is permitted to reign within us. "A good man out of the good treasure of his heart brings forth good things, and an evil man out of the evil treasure brings forth evil things" (Matthew 12:35). What occupies our hearts ultimately governs our actions.

The same is true with our words, " . . . For out of the abundance of the heart the mouth speaks" (Matthew 12:34). Cheerful words and joyful deeds expose a happy heart. On the contrary, sarcasm and defensiveness reveal a bitter heart. 1 Samuel 2:3 admonishes, "Talk no more so very proudly; let no arrogance come from your mouth, for the LORD is the God of knowledge; and by Him actions are weighed." Good or evil, right or wrong, our actions speak and so do our creative endeavors. They not only take on our personalities in style, but also in substance, representing our nature as well as our purpose. When people look at our lives or consider the contents of our artistic expression they should see that *which is good*, because God is good.

I'm not talking about removing conflict, contrast, or competition; but rather demonstrating good and promoting hope through the things we produce. For example, I could paint a dark and dreary scene of the ravages of war, leaving the viewer bewildered. However, if I add a lamppost or a light in a window, no matter how dim or insignificant it may seem, hope emanates. It's not about avoiding reality, but how we portray reality that matters.

God's Expression Here on Earth

Because we are not instantly made perfect upon accepting Jesus into our lives, it does not seem we could ever do God justice in our portrayal of Him. However, He still calls us to be His visible expression here on earth; we should take every care to make sure we represent Him well.

You are the light of the world. A city that is set on a hill cannot be hidden. Nor do they light a lamp and put it under a basket, but on a lamp stand, and it gives light to all who are in the house. Let your light so shine before men, that they may see your good works and glorify your Father in heaven. (Matthew 5:14–16)

As we learned in Chapter One, God introduced Himself to Creation as Light. Furthermore, He established this light in purity and truth. "And God saw the light, that it was good . . ." (Genesis 1:4). James 1:17–18 tells us,

Every good gift and every perfect gift is from above, and comes down from the Father of lights, with whom there is no varia- tion or shadow of turning. Of His own will He brought us forth by the word of truth, that we might be a kind of first fruits of His creatures.

God is the Father of lights and He reproduces after His own kind, thus 1 Thessalonians 5:5 calls us "The children of light." When we accept Jesus as our savior, the light of God begins to shine in our lives. Now it's up to us how we will manifest His light to the world. This is where creativity comes in. God wants to use our talents as a means of expressing His multifaceted image through our individual personali- ties. My light will shine differently than your light, but all God asks is that we shine our lights for Him, affecting those who see it for good.

Proverbs 11:30 declares, "The fruit of the righteous is a tree of life, and he who wins souls is wise." We need to pray for direction in how to use our *good and perfect gifts* to reach this lost and dying world. Though creativity benefits us on a personal level through our health and emotional well-being, God's intention for the arts goes beyond personal gain. We can use our talents as a means of attracting atten- tion, causing others to see, hear, think, and feel, thus opening doors of opportunity to witness.

Religion, without relationship, does not appeal to most. People who do not know Jesus personally cannot fathom a tangible relation- ship with the Creator of the universe, although this has always been His primary objective. His secondary goal was to make us unique and to give purpose to our lives. None of us are an accident, nor have our talents come to us by chance. Therefore, we should take the gifts of God seriously and use them for His glory.

Because we're all different, we must take into consideration that what works to bring some to salvation will not work for others. Finding what will reach each soul is where God utilizes our tools of individuality and creativity. It will take more than one light to shine forth the truth in love. My light cannot penetrate every heart and neither will yours, but together we can share the gospel around the world.

Making Right Choices

Knowing God's will and obeying it can, at times, be two completely different things. One way to make it easier involves keeping ungodly influences at bay, including what we *allow* ourselves to see and hear. In Genesis 2, we find Adam and Eve living in a perfect world with everything they needed to enjoy life to the fullest—yet with one stipulation: "Do not eat from the tree of the Knowledge of Good and Evil" (Genesis 2:17). The scenario changes in Genesis 3, where we find Eve looking at the one and only enticement off limits to them. She was also listening to what the serpent had to say about the possibilities if she ate. She "saw the tree was good for food" and that it was "pleasant to the eyes" (Genesis 3:6). Eve took herself out of a place of safety when she willingly chose to focus on the temptation. James 1:14–15 is very clear, "But each one is tempted when he is drawn away by his own desires and enticed. Then when desire has conceived, it gives birth to sin; and sin, when it is full-grown, brings forth death."

1 Samuel 13:14 speaks of David as being a man after God's own heart and his reputation praiseworthy; however, one day he let down his guard and allowed his eyes to wander. It was during the time "when kings go forth to battle" (2 Samuel 11:1). He sent Joab, the Captain of the Guard in his place. That night he couldn't sleep so he decided to take a walk upon the rooftop, where he looked, desired, and fell into adultery with Bathsheba (2 Samuel 11). When David looked, he saw the obvious, a beautiful young woman bathing—but what he didn't *see* was the result of holding his gaze longer than he should have.

Seeing the beautiful woman wasn't sin. Sometimes we can't control what comes into our sight, but we can control our response. David should have quickly turned and walked away. Unfortunately, that's not what happened.

Thankfully, we serve a God of second chances, where true repentance paves the way for God to cleanse our hearts. However, each one of us is accountable for the things we say and do. Philippians 2:12 says, " . . . work out your own salvation with fear and trembling" implying a continued effort on our part. Proverbs 4:25 tells us, "Let your eyes look straight ahead, and your eyelids look right before you." Even David said in Psalm 101:3, "I will set nothing wicked before my eyes," because he knew what would happen if he did. If we allow our eyes to wander and behold the unclean, or our ears to hear perversion and lies, impure thoughts will come—all too often resulting in immoral behaviors.

Continual communication with Jesus and His word is imperative. This keeps our relationship strong so we won't be caught off guard in a vulnerable place where godly behavior and good creativity begins to die. If we fall into sin, it taints our witness. Jesus forgives when we repent, but people have a tendency to remember our words and actions, and there will always be those who are quick to condemn. This alone should encourage us to maintain our integrity by living within the boundaries and protection of God's word. "That you may become blameless and harmless, children of God without fault in the midst of a crooked and perverse generation, among whom you shine as lights in the world" (Philippians 2:15). "Therefore, beloved, looking forward to these things, be diligent to be found by Him in peace, without spot and blameless" (2 Peter 3:14). "That you may approve the things that are excellent, that you may be sincere and without offense till the day of Christ, being filled with the fruits of righteousness which are by Jesus Christ, to the glory and praise of God" (Philippians 1:10–11). We are God's art, put on display for the world to see Jesus through us. May we live with integrity, worthy of His name.

Holding the Line

There is more to living right than keeping ungodly influences at bay. Psalm 89:14 tells us, "Righteousness and justice are the foundation of Your throne; mercy and truth go before Your face." These foundations are Biblical guidelines wherewith we construct moral standards. "If the foundations are destroyed, what can the righteous do?" (Psalm 11:3). We must maintain our integrity and defend our godly heritage.

Jesus prayed in John 17:15, "I do not pray that You should take them out of the world, but that You should keep them from the evil one." This does not give us permission to be a recluse, separating ourselves from the world and avoiding secular things. It means letting our light shine in the darkness and learning how to create through a godly proactive attitude. Proverbs 4:18 tells us, "But the path of the just is like the shining sun, that shines ever brighter unto the perfect day." This is how we should see ourselves. Even more, this is how the world should see us. Yet we must be ever mindful that there will be things that attempt to lure us outside of God's protection. If we acknowledge our weaknesses and avoid these temptations, we will overcome. Obedience to God's word is a refuge, conducive to godly observation, godly thought, and godly deeds. 2 Timothy 3:16–17 admonishes, "All Scripture is given by inspiration of God, and is profitable for doctrine, for reproof, for correction, for instruction in righteousness, that the man of God may be complete, thoroughly equipped for every good work."

God, through His creation, provided everything that humanity would need to be creative and productive. Consequently, an abundance of great and useful things exists in our world today. Yet, at the same time, many inventions have been destructive or used for personal gain, even at the cost of hurting others and degrading society. Creativity and every form of art can have a positive influence, inspiring and blessing people's lives. Unfortunately, the same arts can be used for evil, seduction, and harm.

1 Timothy 6:10 warns, "For the love of money is the root of all evil . . ." (KJV). Many have fallen into the trap of creating what will sell, compromising integrity for monetary gain, selling their souls for the riches of this world. There is nothing wrong with being successful and making money as long as morality is preserved. The Apostle Paul instructed Timothy saying, "Let no one despise your youth, but be an example to the believers in word, in conduct, in love, in spirit, in faith, in purity" (1Timothy 4:12). We should be present day examples of this verse, making us viable participants in proclaiming the Good News of Jesus Christ and letting our lights shine through the arts.

Mood Swings

We discovered in Chapter One that each of us has an intrinsic creative nature. How we express this nature is as much of who we are as the art itself. Therefore, when we produce art during an emotional slump it will undoubtedly reflect the tone of our mood. The same is true when on an emotional high—a giddy disposition will manifest itself much differently than a somber attitude and so forth.

More often than not, mood swings are temporary and don't generate life changes. However, if our thoughts or emotions change for any length of time, the result becomes evident in all areas of life. For example, consider someone who excels when complimented. What happens when he/she takes a high stress job where it seems impossible to live up to expectations because of constant criticism? Confidence wanes and either productivity decreases or anxiety fills every action. It won't be long before the effects alter responses outside the work place as well. Even spending time at a creative outlet will be difficult because the pressure to perform spills over into everything and becomes a dominate factor.

Another illustration: suppose on the thoroughfare of life something goes wrong and a situation overtakes us. What happens during the season of confusion or negative sentiment? Should all creative action stop because the manifestation of our emotions might not rightly represent the heart of God? The answer depends upon how our creative energies are used and yet, keeping stress, depression, disorders, or any other kind of hurtful situation internalized can be detrimental.

Let's consider some possible consequences if one's rationale remains out of focus. To release feelings through depressed or violent music, or gory or perverted art, is not the release we are looking for. No edification ensues from such actions. These things merely feed the negative, intensify hurt, and fortify walls of defense around a wounded heart. This kind of creative output is *not* good! Then if taken public, it drags others into the degradation, causing them to be negatively influenced by someone else's pain.

The world teaches it's okay to vent, but destructive art cannot bring about healing or restoration. Ephesians 4:26 says, "Be angry, and do not sin: do not let the sun go down on your wrath." Anger, when not kept in check, is dangerous, and opposes God's purpose for creative expression. Nevertheless, if we use creative outlets to get our minds off the negative, good things can happen. After hearing Jake perform a piano solo, his father told me how music was a good release for his son and that he often played as a way to express his emotions. Then he explained that the piece his son composed for the concert was the culmination of a year full of highs and lows. It started with him having a girlfriend and everything going well, he loved his music and his life. But things became bleak when he suffered a disappointing break-up, causing frustration and mood swings. Eventually, things got better; he poured himself into his music, met a sweet girl, and was happy again. Now his composition made sense—it started calmly, picked up in intensity, and then reached a point of harsh discord. After a time, it began to soften and returned to a pleasant sounding melody. In this case, his musical involvement helped him to handle the ups and downs of life without overstepping godly boundaries.

Creativity is a powerful tool, used in so many ways, both privately and publicly. That's why we must "Test all things; hold fast what is good" (1 Thessalonians 5:21). If discouragement looms, we can pray as David did, "Create in me a clean heart oh God and renew a right spirit within me." Prayer initiates the recovery process by healing emotions and restoring opportunity for good creativity. The Psalmist often turned to his creative outlet during times of despair, and it always brought him to a place of hope and rejoicing.

Portraying Purpose

Though a drawing consists of lines, lines can only tell part of the story. The steady hand of an experienced artist taught me this lesson while watching him sketch a young woman. He quickly outlined the face, adding each feature with such ease, every line precise. It took only a few moments to capture the woman's likeness and yet it seemed ordinary and uninviting. While pondering why, I continued to observe as he began to add shading and highlights. What a difference this made; the face took on depth and a luster that made it more life-like. Still something was missing, but what was it? Before I had time to think about the answer, the artist began using his fingers and proceeded to smudge some of the rough edges, causing them to look softer. Lines disappeared into smooth even shading and the face seemed to come alive; I could feel the smile as well as see it. The highlights in her eyes not only revealed the light source, but also sparkled with sincerity. It was as if the artist's rendering captured the woman's vibrant personality; the finished sketch made her look like someone you would like to meet.

I have seen other portraits, however, that were so stark it made me wonder if the person's demeanor was really that sharp and it gave me an uneasy feeling. If a drawing can make us think, feel, or respond in different ways, how much more should we realize our lives cause a response—good, bad, or indifferent—where people form judgments of us by the impression we leave with them upon our meeting. Our personalities and how we represent ourselves make a difference in how others receive us. We could be fantastic authors, artists, musicians, etc., but if the sharpness of our behavior or the image we portray turns people off, it will close at least some doors of opportunity. I learned this through experience. I have all the characteristics of a friendly outgoing person, but in the past my rough edges manifested and others witnessed this weakness. The result: there were those who didn't hold their gaze long enough to see the softer side of me and for them, I lost my ability to minister and/or to serve.

Unfortunately, some situations don't offer us a second chance; that's why it's of utmost importance we take heed to our mannerisms and allow the Spirit of God to soften our edges. We are God's art and He brings adjustments. The smudging, blending, and smoothing out of our coarse tendencies can cause life to get a little blurry, even bringing pain at times. We may even want God to pull back His finger and call it "good enough" on the painting of our lives, but we must trust that He knows best. "Now no chastening seems to be joyful for the present, but painful; nevertheless, afterward it yields the peaceable fruit of righteousness to those who have been trained by it" (Hebrews 12:11). If we get lost in the moment and forget His dealings are for our own good, we won't allow Him to achieve the *detail* He desires whereby making us someone people would like to meet and the witnesses He expects us to be.

The artist who did the drawing of the young woman could have chosen to leave the edges rough, a stylistic preference; but his purpose of showing us the radiance of youth would not have been accomplished by doing so. He made a statement by tempering her features; the finished piece represented his intention. Hereby I pose a question: Does the art in this case characterize the artist or the woman portrayed? The woman is clearly recognizable, and the artist's style obvious; both are needed to accomplish the anticipated goal, right? Yet the fame goes *not* to the woman, but to the artist who put her on display! Even so, God has an objective and, allowing His artistic touch to permeate our lives generates opportunity for Him to display His objective, which is to reveal His righteous nature through us.

An ambassador does not come representing himself or his own

opinions, but the ideals of the nation from whence he was sent. Accordingly, we must keep ourselves within all the boundaries of God's word, understanding that we are His ambassadors to a lost and dying world. In our lives and through our creative expression, may we show forth the image of God.

chapter eleven

expression and experience

According to the eternal purpose which He accomplished in Christ Jesus our Lord, in whom we have boldness and access with confidence through faith in Him. Ephesians 3:11–12

One of the summer art classes offered by a local college was to be held at a park on the Long Island Sound. The course description consisted of four paintings, each done from the same location. After the students chose their setting, they were to try different techniques, color combinations, and individual expression. The only requirement for the class was to make sure all four paintings looked different from each other, even though the scene remained the same. When Neal heard about the course, he thought it sounded interesting and decided to attend.

After surveying the park, Neal chose to paint one of the gazebos that overlooked the bay. His first two paintings were artistically sound, but his professor wanted him to be more expressive, to take command of the subject matter. He suggested Neal enhance what he saw by taking off personal restraints and infusing emotion into his work. Having considered this advice, Neal arrived at the next class with a skip in his step and ready to tackle his assignment with new vigor. He set up his easel, got out his supplies, and started to paint. In the meantime, two young women came along and sat on a bench within earshot. They talked loudly, obviously disturbed by a situation that seemed to grow worse as the conversation continued. Neal couldn't help but hear the women talk; yet his location couldn't change because of the class assignment. It wasn't long before the women's prolonged venting began to irritate him. The next thing he knew it was showing up in his painting; the objects became abstract and the colors stark. Without a doubt, this painting looked completely different from the first two. A sense of agitation dominated the painting though it had nothing to do with the view or the serenity of the day. Plainly, his expressed mood was a direct result of an internal response to an external distraction.

When his professor saw the painting, he was quite impressed with the contrast. Neal explained what brought about the drastic change and how he projected his frustrations onto the canvas. The painting clearly illustrates what can happen when personal sentiments are included. This wasn't the most enjoyable way to become expressive, but it worked. Mood, along with a wide range of emotions will strengthen our art when appropriately combined.

My commercial art teacher in high school taught a very controlled method of drawing, which limited artistic expression. Looking back at my early pieces, they were very stiff and lacked energy. When we add mood and emotion to our subjects, it communicates a stronger and more reflective form of art, which is much more effective than merely copying what we see. The same is true for music. It's like going to a jazz concert and hearing the musicians' *adlib*. This not only shows off their skill, but an authentic passion emanates from them as their music draws the audience in—thus enhancing the moment and making the experience more enjoyable, as well as memorable.

Recently our family attended the local high school musical. The performance was nicely choreographed and came together without incident, yet something was lacking. Mentioning this to my husband, he noted that some of the actors did not "get into" their roles. Yes, they *did* and *said* all the right things, but it was more mechanical than spontaneous. In the midst of this, however, there were those who performed with style; willing to showboat their parts, bringing emotion in and through the characters they portrayed. Why did some of them go beyond doing it right to doing it remarkably well? Because they were able to put aside all fear and restraint to feel and become the part. Freedom of expression made all the difference.

Maintaining Balance

We must keep things in perspective and maintain a godly balance when expressing our moods. Not everything in life, or even in creativity for that matter, will be enjoyable; yet we shouldn't continually be in a state of discontentment or gloom. People often form their opinions of us by three specific things: our actions, the integrity of our words, and the disclosure of our temperament. Because of this, we must not allow ourselves to be stuck in a melancholy or "woe is me" mode. When this happens, we observe little, productive thoughts are few, and our actions have no positive influence. Everything becomes darkened by a general lack of hope.

Sullen mannerisms are hard to hide, and if they become commonplace, they hurt our witness for Jesus. That is why we must control our emotions, especially negative ones. Everyone has gone through tough times or been in difficult situations. Some handle it well, while others seem trapped; but it's imperative that our attitude, appearance, and approach shift from discouragement to emotional stability. Some of you may be asking, "But how do I get there?" It begins by having a genuine trust that God controls our circumstances and that He has our best interest in mind, even if those circumstances seem confusing at times. Jeremiah 29:11 puts it this way, "For I know the thoughts that I think toward you, says the LORD, thoughts of peace and not of evil, to give you a future and a hope." Psalm 56:9 encourages, "When I cry out to You, then my enemies will turn back; this I know, because God is for me." Then we must live as if we believe God's word is true.

If you're stuck in a less than charming world and don't feel very motivated, put your creative outlet to work and watch how it changes your mood. Maybe you're in a season where creative ideas are few and far between. This could cause you to ignore your outlet instead of reaching for inspiration beyond how you feel. If this is the case, don't fear; all artists go through dry seasons similar to what we experience in our walk with God. When this happens spiritually, we don't ignore God, but fight through the languorous emotions until we find times of refreshing. This should also be true when it comes to art; sometimes we need to fight off the doldrums instead of giving in to them.

Emotional slumps often hit people during the dreary months of winter. Some call it cabin fever and they just can't wait for spring. None of us can change the seasons, but we can rid ourselves of discouragement by taking action. One way to do so is by taking our art in a different direction. For example, if you draw with precision, do a loose abstract piece just for the fun of it; or if you always paint landscapes, try tackling a still-life. If you quilt, pick fabrics you wouldn't have chosen before and let the colors inspire you. If you enjoy making music, experiment with different sounds—be passionate. If you're always serious while writing, comically describe a funny situation. It doesn't have to be long, but it should make you laugh. Doing something out of the norm or taking extreme measures can initiate an emotional breakthrough. This doesn't mean all your art will remain out of character, it's just good to occasionally step away from your routine and experiment. It keeps things interesting and you will find it rejuvenates your creative enthusiasm.

I'll never forget the time I was working on a watercolor of an old barn. The painting had some good qualities but lacked energy.

So, in a very uncharacteristic manner, I drastically loosened up the background by adding a tempestuous sky. This gave the painting a feeling of an approaching storm. What a difference it made—not only in the painting, but also in me. I went from feeling discouraged to feeling fantastic all because this audacious step turned ordinary into interesting. To risk ruining a painting that was otherwise finished was unprecedented for me, but I found it liberating. Though this may seem simple, it became significant because it altered my artistic approach from that point forward. It also made me realize I could be more daring and confident about other things as well.

Sometimes we just need to break out of the mode and allow the process to carry us. I like to compare it to developing a photograph; at first, it's a little blurry and we're not sure what we'll uncover, but as the process continues, the picture becomes clear. Even so, with the arts, we shouldn't be surprised when bold participation augments the creative process and our skill increases. The results of these actions will encourage us to delve even further into the innovative challenges that lay before us. As our outlets improve and gain in momentum, they will also take on a greater ability to affect our audience.

It is important to make time for creative growth because the benefits go beyond art. Confidence emerges and boldness becomes evident in other areas of our lives. When we allow for freedom of expression, the light of individuality beams brightly, adding dynamics to what was once ordinary.

If diving right into an artistic endeavor seems too drastic or challenging at this point because of emotional weariness or outside pressures, try visiting an art gallery or museum and allow others' art to energize you. Going to a play or concert can help you step outside yourself, where new thoughts and feelings can arise. Quilting displays or craft shows are usually available most of the year. Choose something you enjoy and be inspired. You don't even have to participate in a creative action at this point; the sights and sounds of others can simply be enough. Yet, while observing the artistic expressions of others, open your heart to see how this can lift you emotionally and stimulate you to start a project of your own. Taking action does wonders for the melancholy heart and others will notice the change in your countenance before you even tell them why. They'll see it in your eyes and in your smile. Your fresh and optimistic appearance will also improve your ability to witness for the Lord.

Communicate Through Your Art

The arts reach into our psyche and induce thoughts and emotions that we wouldn't otherwise have. Why do you suppose retailers play the kinds of music they do? Because it creates an atmosphere for buying, making the appropriate age group feel comfortable in their store. Brightly colored billboards line highways and flashy advertisements fill magazines, all intended to increase sales of their products. Our world has become dependent upon visual and audio stimulants. The mere fact that this is a reality proves the arts speak.

The walls of most rooms display some form of art (including photography) and music is readily available throughout the day. The kinds of art we hang in our homes or offices can tell us a lot about each other: what we like, how we think, and often what we believe. The same is true with the kinds of music we enjoy. Taking this a step further, as artists, we can use our outlets to convey more than mere talent, by infusing ideals into the things we produce. By doing so, we have the ability to help others through their day.

How often do you have a song running through your head because you heard it first thing in the morning? We probably all do this more than we realize. The melody catches our attention and then it has the ability to affect our moods. Even the lyrics can make a difference in our temperaments and influence our responses depending on whether the words are uplifting or negative. This is also true concerning the things we observe, bringing us back to the importance of creating that which is good. Art has the power to communicate with its audience; therefore, we are accountable for the message our creative outlets convey. "So then each of us shall give account of himself to God. Therefore let us not judge one another anymore, but rather resolve this, not to put a stumbling block or a cause to fall in our brother's way" (Romans 14:12–13).

The arts can bring a sense of tranquility and hope. For example, I've been in waiting rooms at medical facilities where it was evident that the person who decorated the room took into consideration the pain or stress that many people feel while there. The choice of art helped to soothe or at least temporally distract patients from their ailments. Strangely enough, these paintings increased my confidence in the doctor's ability. But I have also been in medical facilities where no creative effort was put forth. Cheap and uneventful prints were sparsely hung in a very cold and clinical manner. This too gave me an opinion about the physician and, even though the art in waiting rooms has nothing to do with a doctor's skill, it can definitely affect our moods and expectations.

Art holds influence and it doesn't have to be on a wall. Have you ever noticed the amount of clothing that displays words, logos, or artwork? These all speak an opinion about something. The most common ones promote a brand of clothing, endorse a favorite team, express allegiance to a certain school or university, or depict a choice vacation spot. The designers promote more than a style of clothing; the artwork is an additional voice or advertisement for the product or location represented.

People support what they believe. Once it goes past the above-mentioned advertisements, there are forms of art used on clothing—some are quite evil and carry satanic connotations. However, we can promote positive ethics to help counteract the dark and destructive ones. Clothing that advances the gospel of Jesus Christ is one way we can use the arts for God. Nevertheless, we must make sure our lifestyles line up with the message; otherwise, we become a reproach. "That you may approve the things that are excellent, that you may be sincere and without offense till the day of Christ" (Philippians 1:10). Godly character matters. We cannot preach the gospel and live the opposite if we want be a good witness for the Lord. Styles of clothing also have a voice: they cry trendy, seductive, radical, conservative, elegant, corporate, sporty, etc. People can read into our personalities and discover what we endorse by how we dress. If our clothing is risqué, that will speak louder than anything we say, even if our words are good. Once others notice the contradiction, it causes them to turn a deaf ear our way. Nevertheless, if the *image* we convey lines up with our words, even if others are uncomfortable with our message, they will be more apt to listen.

Art Speaks

Whether we create the art or simply choose the art, it's our opportunity to communicate. For that reason, we must take into consideration what elements are vital to having art speak.

First, no matter what we produce or decide upon, it must captivate the beholder. Artists can use color, lighting, and strong design to help lead one's eye in and around a piece of art. Elements can be larger or smaller than normal, put in the wrong place, or even eliminated if so desired. For example, a face with no eyes may imply the person is physically blind, spiritually blind, or maybe blinded by circumstance. The conclusion may differ for each person who sees it and other objects in the piece can help lead to the intended response, but the mere fact there are *no* eyes will catch people's attention, causing most to ponder why, which opens a window for the artist to make a point.

Many portrait artists prefer their subject to sit for them instead of working from a photograph; this way they can pick up on the person's mannerisms as they draw or paint. By doing so, a mood or a look that reflects the person's nature can be incorporated, giving you a taste of their personality, along with their physical appearance.

Secondly, having passion for what we do affects our determination and influences our actions. We will be more apt to think about what we want to create and why before getting started, ultimately making a difference in the finished product. My sister-in-law, Nancy, enjoys sewing original quilts for family members and close friends. Special occasions often include a new quilt coinciding with the event. Her thoughtful planning and exuberance turn her gifts into keepsakes that hold lasting value and memories.

Thirdly, and most importantly, our art must have clear purpose. It matters not that we can catch one's attention or even display a passion for that matter—if we do not have something constructive to exhibit, or if what we create comes across as vague. Just as authors must have a topic and a detailed goal in order to successfully share their message, so it is true for all the arts to be effective. A trumpet has a distinct sound and is easily recognizable, but in the hands of a skilled musician, specific emotions can ensue, even causing our moods to change. In the days of old, the trumpet had several objectives; it gave one sound to call the men together for battle, a different tone meant retreat. There was a tune for the call to worship and a dirge for a time of mourning.

Even things without life, whether flute or harp, when they make a sound, unless they make a distinction in the sounds, how will it be known what is piped or played? For if the trumpet makes an uncertain sound, who will prepare for battle? (1 Corinthians 14:7–8)

Every sound or melody had a direct purpose so the people knew to take the correct action. Each of our creative outlets has the ability to affect those we reach; the ultimate impact depends upon the clarity and extent of our purpose.

To produce successful art, we must incorporate the appropriate mood to correspond with its intention. For example, if a song is to express happiness but most of the notes are played in minors, it will mislead the audience and the objective of joy will not be achieved. But if the goal were one of grief, the same tune would be suitable and affectively move those who hear. Furthermore, the arts have the ability to alter our moods and change how we think or feel about issues. Immediately after 9–11, songs with a patriotic theme were very popular and those who chose to sing them had a platform to be heard.

A new wave of patriotic paintings, sculptures, and poetry surfaced as well, renewing the nation's hope during a dark hour. The more our art has purpose, the more influence it will have over those it reaches.

We must also bear in mind that the things we produce have the power to motivate or discourage, to give hope or leave a feeling of bleakness, to cause laughter or bring tears. Each of the arts has its own language and communicates to both the conscious and subconscious of mankind. For instance, I've had teenagers tell me they can't stand the silence; they must have music playing, even while studying for a test. They have conditioned themselves to need noise to be comfortable in their surroundings. This isn't necessarily a bad thing. If the choice of music edifies, the effect will be for good. But if the music and its lyrics are degrading, violent, or inappropriately sensual, this too has an impact, adding to the deterioration of a generation.

Some believe if you can change a nation's music and art, that the philosophy or lifestyle of that society will follow. I would have to agree, because in our nation's case, both music and art drastically shifted directions in the sixties and the results have since mushroomed and become very evident. For all we've gained in civil liberties and freedom of speech, we've lost in the lowering of moral standards, gangs, rising crime rates, corporate scandals, greed, rampant STD's, and internet spamming to name a few. By embracing humanism, many have added to the problem by trying to eliminate God—because if there is no God, then there is no conviction for immoral behaviors and every one is free to do what's right in their own eyes. Yet by taking action, we can alter this course. We cannot afford to sit back and do nothing. We must use our freedom of expression (while we still have it) to promote that which is good and get involved in the many powerful forms of communication. Darkness did not spring up over night and our light may not seem that effective at first, but if we will be faithful to get involved, God will be faithful to use our talents for His glory. Many Christians have been lulled to sleep by complacency, but I am confident that as we take action, our efforts will make a difference. Even a small stone cast into water will make ripples!

The Personal Touch

The most effective sermons a pastor ever preaches are the ones that have touched him personally. The content of his message grows in merit because experience accentuates his knowledge of the word and his examples become tangible to the congregation. Imparting human sentiments along with experience gives our creative outlets a pulse, supplying mood, expression, and interest. Art doesn't need to be complicated to move people, but it should contain direction, passion, and purpose. Begin with an end in mind—your goal, then just as a pastor does, pray for wisdom in how to accomplish your objective and watch how God's inspiration flows into your creative outlet and out to your audience.

Very seldom (not counting mass productions) is art done without the evidence of our personalities. When I paint, no one else is around; it's just me in my studio experiencing the power of expression. When finished, I can show others the results of my effort and, if they look past the initial glance, they will see a part of me. They will also know something about my personality, even if we've never met. If we walk through a gallery where the work of various artists is on display, we will find the styles and subject matter as diverse as the artists themselves. Some of the pieces will be loose or abstract, while others photo realistic; the rest undoubtedly, fill the vast range in between. But each will be true to the artist's personality because the development of creativity, like so many things in God, begins internally and then becomes an external extension of who we are.

Having taught a number of art classes, I look forward to picking up on the disposition of each student. Generally, I have a good idea by the end of our first lesson together. It's easy to recognize the perfectionists; they expect great things from themselves, usually immediately. Most are very determined, yet some frustrate easily. Then there are those who like bold color and contrast; they are very out-going, daring, and willing to try new things. I've had others who favor pastel colors and a softer appeal; they quite often have a quiet or shy demeanor. Individual characteristics will, and rightly should, be an active part of our creative outlet.

When picking a subject to draw, paint, or sculpt, or a theme for a composition or a song, we usually choose one that has more meaning to us than the artwork. I am more apt to draw one of my nieces than to draw a little girl I do not know, or do a painting of a place I have actually been rather than using a photograph of a place I've never visited. If I don't have a specific place to paint, I will find a picture of something that interests me, such as a seascape. When I make a quilt, I choose fabrics and a pattern that appeal to me. I'll write poetry about something relevant to what I'm going through. I've even done paintings for people who requested a style of art that did not reflect my personality; yet my mannerisms were still evident in the finished product. Our nature will flow through our creative outlets—the two are inseparable. When art contains personal experiences, the outcome has greater opportunity to make an impact on our audience. It's all part of God's purpose for individuality and His plan to speak through us as we use our talents for Him.

Keep in mind, expression alone is not enough. We may be able to tell someone is a perfectionist without knowing what he/she believes or wherein his/her passion lies. This is where we can take our creative outlet to another level of communication, especially when we allow our art to be inspired by God. The next chapter deals with using our talents as a way to open doors to share the gospel of Jesus Christ.

chapter twelve

purpose beyond us

*This is a faithful saying, and these things I want you
to affirm constantly, that those who have believed in
God should be careful to maintain good works. These
things are good and profitable to men. Titus 3:8*

The message art conveys can be very strong. Yet, in many instances, the message has been one of degradation. We live in a society that claims to be progressive, where anything goes, and many progressive thinkers have no problem preaching their gospel of immorality and situational ethics through the arts. Behaviors once considered a reproach are now commonplace because the unregenerate took a stand for their cause and their voice became louder than the voice of righteousness. Entertainment, for example, has become quite seductive by steadily displaying lowered moral values. We must not overlook the fact that art speaks. "There are, it may be, so many kinds of languages in the world, and none of them is without significance" (1 Corinthians

14:10). These voices can be good or bad, right or wrong, and our silence or unwillingness to participate in a positive light has allowed darkness to dominate culture and art.

Parts of society even want to intimidate and silence the Christian voice by preaching *tolerance.* But their idea of tolerance would, in many cases, simply compromise moral standards in order to choose ungodly lifestyles without guilt—blind to the fact that their day of reckoning will come. If we surrender to this pressure, it renders us powerless while we silently and willingly watch people die without hope. However, the gospel of Jesus Christ can be preached in love, without condoning sin. As Christians, we should be more concerned about winning souls than being *politically correct.* It's time to become godly activists, eager to combat irreverent voices with art inspired by the Creator Himself.

Jesus gave us gifts and talents to gain entry into peoples' hearts, but to do so, we must take heed to Romans 12:2, "And do not be conformed to this world, but be transformed by the renewing of your mind, that you may prove what is that good and acceptable and perfect will of God." When transformation becomes important to us—to be and act more like God and less like the world—we will walk in confidence and be enabled to display godly character through the arts.

This does not mean everything we create needs a Christian theme. For example, romantic novels can be written without including promiscuity, though it's a contemporary trend. A while back, my thirteen-year-old daughter started to read a popular novel to me and I was appalled to find the author had the newly acquainted characters engage in sex before the end of the first chapter. Sadly, this has become acceptable because society has been flooded with the idea that it's okay. And why not? It's the easier road; it takes no backbone to compromise moral standards. Matthew 7:13 puts it this way, "Enter by the narrow gate; for wide is the gate and broad is the way that leads to destruction, and there are many who go in by it." Romans 12:21 adds, "Do not be overcome by evil, but overcome evil with good." We can counter this ungodly trend through the arts; such as writing love stories that promote the importance of friendship first and reveal the truth that *lasting* relationships are built on love and commitment—not uncontrolled lust.

Creative actions exist in an array of forms and carry a diverse range of intentions. Some of it simply represents personal preference, while others deliberately convey a philosophy. We must learn how to edify with our creative outlet, causing people to think positively by reinforcing that which is good. There are enough negative and anti-Christian voices in the world today. It's time we use our talents, no matter what form or style we choose, to speak life and promote integrity for the greater good.

Divine Inspiration

The arts can be used to fill our world with sights and sounds that bring glory to our Maker and draw people unto salvation. To do this, we must learn how to make our form of art speak, going beyond our natural senses to see and hear with our hearts and act through our beliefs. "But there is a spirit in man, and the breath of the Almighty gives him understanding" (Job 32:8). God gave humanity the ability to think and act creatively beyond mere instincts. Part of this ability includes the supernatural where the plant and animal worlds have no part, a divine interaction between God and man. "And the LORD God formed man of the dust of the ground, and breathed into his nostrils the breath of life; and man became a living being" (Genesis 2:7), thus taking on "the image of God" (Genesis 1:27). When God made man, he was perfectly formed, yet without life. Then God breathed into man and he came alive. The word *breath* in Hebrew is *nshamah* and part of its definition means *divine inspiration.* Man not only became a living soul, this divine connection gave him the capacity to receive guidance and to communicate with his Maker on a personal level.

Unfortunately, since the *fall of man* we no longer live in that perfect state of divine inspiration; therefore, much of what is produced does not represent God's image nor His will. Salvation reopens the lines of communication and gives us opportunity again to receive insight and direction from the Almighty. The effects of this relationship should show up in our actions, as God weaves His purpose in and through our lives.

Proverbs 29:18 tells us, "Where there is no revelation, the people cast off restraint . . ." God desires to give us dreams and visions, to breathe upon us; whereby revealing His purpose for a cause that reaches beyond us. Once His redemption infuses our being, it unleashes our spirits to receive creative direction; "For it is God who works in you both to will and to do for His good pleasure" (Philippians 2:13). But we must be willing to seek His face and make ourselves available to hear His voice.

> *For this reason we also, since the day we heard it, do not cease to pray for you, and to ask that you may be filled with the knowledge of His will in all wisdom and spiritual understanding; that you may walk worthy of the Lord, fully pleasing Him, being fruitful in every good work and increasing in the knowledge of God. (Colossians 1:9–10)*

We are the avenue He has chosen to fulfill His purposes here on earth and one way to achieve His objective is to use our talents in promoting the good news of Jesus Christ.

Our godly influence will be limited if we don't look for divine inspiration, because it minimizes our opportunities to use our talents for His glory. Creative thinking gives us wings to fly and propels us beyond the ordinary, but walking in the light of God's word adds eternal purpose to our actions. It's time to start looking at our artistic expressions as tools to share the gospel.

As I talked to a young pastor about the need for creative outlets, he agreed wholeheartedly and interjected how having one helped him emotionally. His response caught my attention so I asked him what his outlet was. He replied with enthusiasm, "Preaching!" He loves studying God's word and thinking of innovative ways to hold his congregation's interest; then he mixes his ideas with his outgoing personality to make his sermons come alive. I thought this a neat correlation, how he associated preaching with creativity and yet, we are not all called to preach from a church pulpit. Nevertheless, each of us can effectively share the gospel within our own sphere of influence by using our God-given talents.

What we create may not specifically have anything to do with Jesus, but it can open doors to witness. Consider Thomas Kinkade, for example: the style and radiance of his paintings attract people to his art. This opens doors for him to share his testimony and boldly declare his faith in Jesus. Art doesn't have to depict Biblical scenes to witness. In Kinkade's case, his paintings bring him popularity, which gives him a platform for people to hear what he has to say.

Another illustration is Joni Eareckson Tada. She became a paraplegic at the age of seventeen and initially thought this was the end of a happy, productive life. Thankfully, God had other plans and she learned to draw with a pencil clenched between her teeth. Because of this remarkable talent, the mastery of her skill opened doors for her to reach a much larger audience. Now, Joni is known the world over; she also sings, writes, and has a great sense of humor—all tools equipping her to reach others for Jesus. Proverbs 17:22 says, "A merry heart does good, like medicine, but a broken spirit dries the bones." Humor uplifts the soul, and is good for us physically as well as emotionally. Unfortunately, even in this, the world has perverted what was once *good* clean fun.

It's all about meeting people where they are and using familiarity as a drawing point. Ron's creative outlet is building and maintaining his racecar. When guys from the community come over to his garage to talk racing and help him with his car, he always finds a way to bring Jesus into the conversation. Ron has taken something he enjoys to get peoples' attention and then uses it to share the gospel along with his love for racing.

Maria has an eye for making rooms beautiful; she even opened a

Bed & Breakfast, which showcases her talent. While serving her guests and talking room decor or antiques, she is mindful to share her faith as opportunities arise. We need not stereotype what it means to be creative or how to use our talents to witness. My list could continue, but hopefully these illustrations will motivate you to ask God how He can use your talents to increase your opportunities to share the gospel. In Psalm 40:10, David declares, "I have not hidden Your righteousness within my heart; I have declared Your faithfulness and Your salvation; I have not concealed Your lovingkindness and Your truth from the great assembly." May we do the same and boldly declare our faith in Jesus Christ.

Throughout the ages, people have been innovative in preaching the word of God. The Gospel message can be direct or implied. Literary allegories such as John Bunyan's *Pilgrim's Progress* and C.S. Lewis' *Chronicles of Narnia* are perfect examples of ways to catch the reader's attention, whereby planting seeds of salvation. Even Jesus used creative expression in the form of parables as He delivered His sermons. Parables are descriptive narratives illustrating spiritual truths. These stories helped people see pictures in their minds, enhancing their ability to comprehend His message. Jesus also understood the individuality of His audience, so each parable reached a specific group of people. Some were presented to farmers, *The Sower and the Seed* and *The Wheat and the Tares*. Others were to the rich, *The Pearl of Great Price* and *The Rich Man and Lazarus*. To the religious Jesus spoke about *The Good Samaritan* and *Cleaning the Outside of the Cup*. Jesus also used visuals to reinforce His teachings: He caused the fig tree to wither, calmed the storm, walked on water, and performed many miracles. These all showed people His divine power and caused them to believe. We may not walk on water, but Jesus promised in John 14:12, "Most assuredly, I say to you, he who believes in Me, the works that I do he will do also; and greater works than these he will do, because I go to My Father."

During the Renaissance, Bible paintings became very popular.

Keep in mind, this era followed the *dark ages* where the light of the gospel had all but gone out. Then the reformation came and with it a wave of visual stimulants, mostly because the people couldn't read. God used these artists to bring the knowledge of salvation to those who didn't know the scriptures. (If you are interested, the book *The Bible and its Painters* compiled by Bruce Bernard, is a wonderful collection of Biblical paintings.) After this period, the desire for the written word came into the hearts of men and God inspired Johann Gutenberg to invent a printing press. What was the first book he printed? The Bible.

Biblical Illustrations

There are examples throughout the Bible where God used people's creative outlets for His purposes. In Exodus 35:30–35, skilled craftsmen made the tabernacle and the things that went therein. In Numbers 21:8–9, God commanded Moses to make a bronze serpent and put it upon a pole. When the people looked at it, they received healing from the venomous snakebites inflicted upon them while in the wilderness.

In 1 Samuel 16, the Spirit of the LORD departed from King Saul because of disobedience and an evil spirit from the LORD troubled him. Saul's torment caused his servants to suggest they find a man who could play skillfully upon the harp. They chose David and as he played a soothing melody, Saul was refreshed and the evil spirit departed from him.

2 Kings 3 tells us about three kings, including Jehoshaphat, king of Judah. They gathered to fight the Moabites, but after a seven day journey, their armies ran out of water. In desperation, the kings called for Elisha the prophet, desiring to hear the word of the Lord. Disturbed by the presence of Jehoram, the ungodly king of Israel, Elisha's annoyance made it difficult for him to hear God's voice; therefore, he requested a minstrel to come and play. As music filled the air, the word of the Lord filled his heart and direction came. Another time, Jehoshaphat sent singers into battle against an invading army and God

wrought a great victory as they praised the beauty of His holiness (2 Chronicles 20:20–21).

The Psalms proclaim words of hope put to music. Proverbs provokes thought, which is good for the creative mind. The Song of Solomon is a beautiful love story written poetically.

God told Jeremiah to go down to the potter's house and there He would speak to him as he watched the potter work with clay (Jeremiah 18:1–10). The potter wasn't doing anything religious, but God still used his creative outlet to show His prophet a spiritual truth.

Both the authors of Ezekiel and Revelation used allegories to share their visions from God. The Bible also contains conflict, adventure, and the individuality of his people; making it a work of art all by itself.

The Arts Possess Purpose Beyond Us

If life offers us no joy or conviction, neither will the things we create. The two go hand in hand and are even more reason to allow God to fill us with His purpose. We have the ability to captivate an audience and should take seriously our chance to impart that which is good, because our creative actions don't stop with us.

We learned in Chapter Three that creativity is a process. That process begins when the seed of creative desire takes hold in our hearts. If you've begun to apply the principles of this book to your life, you most likely found yourself excited and eager to get started. Yet for some of you, apprehension lingers. Emotions come into play and you're not quite sure if your innate creative ability can accomplish all that is stirring in your heart. Fear not, in time your doubts will diminish and your efforts will begin to take shape.

Our first creative attempts may fall short of our aspirations, but remember, talents develop with time and use, so give them a chance to grow. We must take every care to keep our desire stronger than any disappointments that come our way. At first, our objectives may seem more like a distant dream than a fast approaching reality. Yet we shouldn't be surprised when sudden bursts of improvement look us in the face and cheer us on. These are the times when the process propels us to believe success is within our grasp.

As we get closer to showing our talent to the world, we may find anxiety appears with new thoughts such as, "Will my expression be worthwhile, how about appealing? What will others think or say about my creative output?" The thought of going public with our creative outlet can be daunting the first time around . . . or every time we enter a new arena or have a different audience. Even a dinner party can seem intimidating depending upon the guests invited or if it is the first time serving a new entree. These feelings are a natural part of the process.

Finally, a piece is finished and we're excited about the outcome. We found pleasure and fulfillment in producing our form of artwork, but its ultimate purpose cannot be complete without sharing the result with others. Although our form of creative expression reflects our personality, we need to understand that the results of artistic endeavors always extend beyond our final product. Just as our children take on a life and identity of their own and continue to grow and develop apart from us, even so a completed piece of art stands on its own merit. Once the creator rests from his work, the creation speaks for itself. For example, when we hear a song we enjoy, we may say, "Oh, I love this song." Not, "I love this singer," though we may be fond of the musician and like his/her music. Couples often have *a song* (not a musician) that reminds them of their love for one another; the lyrics and melody are what captivate their attention. Do you see how the song has influence apart from and beyond the artist?

This truth follows every form of creative endeavor. A painting can have an effect on us though we know little or nothing about the artist. A quilt can warm us when the quilter is gone, a book can instruct us without the author present. The arts have an ability to move us even after their creator is deceased, because the art lives on separately from the artist, yet bearing his/her image. Our artistic expression can make a difference in the lives of people we've never met; that is why we must create with purpose. And keep in mind, we cannot take anything with us when we die, but we can leave our art and our legacy as an encouragement to those who follow.

Ephesians 4:29 instructs, "Let no corrupt word proceed out of your mouth, but what is good for necessary edification, that it may impart grace to the hearers." It's important that we generate art with a goal in mind, because what we produce interacts with others in much the same way we communicate in person. It's up to us to be mindful that the arts speak and accountability matters; our form of art could live on for many generations. Therefore, our creative expression must bear the stamp of God's approval—that which is good. Once it does, share it with the world and allow God to use it according to His will.

The Need for an Outlet

Another way to explain this principle would be the *inflow* of creative thought and the *outflow* of creative action. Come with me on a journey to the land of Palestine where we find the Sea of Galilee and the beautiful region round about. To the north are the Mountains of Tiberius where fresh springs, rain waters, and melting snow flow into the Jordan River, then into the Sea of Galilee. The Sea freely takes in this fresh water, but also produces and gives out of its resources. Here we have a location with an abundance of life and prosperity, including a booming fishing industry, irrigation systems for vast agricultural growth, large cities, and much commerce. The region also supports tourism and recreation. Beyond these life-producing resources and benefits, which take place because of the on going process of inflow and outflow—the water proceeds back into the Jordan River and flows southward.

As we continue our journey, where does this river end? At the Dead Sea. Here we find a hot, barren land with no large cities, no fishing industry, and no irrigation ditches or agriculture. The only thing we find here are a few resorts so people can come to see the phenomenon of a body of water that produces no life and to float in its extremely salty waters. The Jordan River flows into both Seas, but only the Sea of Galilee has outflow. The Dead Sea has *no outlet* and though it receives fresh water, it stagnates and evaporates, killing all that was once productive.

Likewise, creativity requires an outlet or it will die. Inspiration can flow into our hearts and our desire to be artists can be sincere, but if we don't take action, nothing can come forth. Stagnation produces barrenness and death. Regardless of our talent or skill level, if we are faithful to use our gifts, God will bring increase. But if we don't take the time or put forth the effort to develop our outlet, God's creative purpose for our lives will shrivel up, leaving us to wonder what might have been. And others will never benefit from the fruit God wanted to bring forth from our creative expression.

All about Purpose

Purpose envelops creativity and it flows into all areas of life and culture. Within God's purpose, there are those specifically called to employ their talents for the kingdom of God, directly using their abilities for ministry. For example, though we all should witness, some have the gift of evangelism, using their enthusiasm and boldness as a tool to draw people to salvation. Some teach and preach with striking eloquence, while others use humor, skits, flag/dance routines, and even feats of strength (to mention a few), to help open hearts and minds to hear the gospel. Christian authors have ample opportunity to share their faith and there are those who sing and/or play an instrument with amazing ability, ushering in the presence of the Lord.

With every calling, God supplies the ability. Nevertheless, our talents are not fully developed at birth, or even when we get saved. We must "walk worthy of the calling with which we were called" (Ephesians 4:1), developing our skills through practice and learning. I knew a young man once who felt he had a call on his life to preach the gospel and his pastor agreed. He had great zeal and came to every service just hoping for an opportunity to speak. His chance finally came and he raced forward so quickly that he forgot his Bible. After about ten minutes of rambling, he returned to his seat in grave disappointment. The call alone does not make us able ministers. "Be diligent to present yourself approved to God, a worker who does not need to be ashamed, rightly dividing the word of truth" (2 Timothy 2:15). No matter what form of creative outlet we use, we need to know and apply God's word to our lives. It also takes time and effort to prepare our hearts, as well as our talents, so that when we make ourselves available for God's service, we won't squander the opportunity.

On a broader scale, we may not be *called* to use our gifting at church services, youth gatherings, or other such public events, but that does not excuse us from witnessing. The apostle Paul admonishes in 1 Corinthians 9:22, " . . . I have become all things to all men, that I might by all means save some." Each of us can think of creative ways to use our talents and personalities to be a light to our family, friends, neighbors, and co-workers. Mark 16:15, commonly known as the great commission says, "And He said to them, Go into all the world and preach the gospel to every creature." This verse is a mandate to all who have accepted Jesus Christ into their hearts, not just to the ministers.

My pastor teaches, "One of the best ways to win people to the Lord is to become their friend." Using the arts is a good way to get to know people, be it taking a class together, joining an art club, quilter's guild, or writer's association. These things open doors, and as friendships ensue, opportunities to witness increase.

"But even if our gospel is veiled, it is veiled to those who are perishing, whose minds the god of this age has blinded, who do not believe, lest the light of the gospel of the glory of Christ, who is the image of God, should shine on them" (2 Corinthians 4:3–4). It is advantageous to the lost when we allow God's Spirit to infiltrate our talents, for His purpose always goes beyond us. Therefore, we need to ask Him to show us how to make the greatest impact on a world that is looking for God; that through our creative actions, they will see *the light* and be saved. 1 Peter 2:12 puts it this way: "that . . . they may, by your good works which they observe, glorify God in the day of visitation."

section four
hindrances to creativity

hope for the hurting

chapter thirteen

things we cannot change

And let us not grow weary while doing good, for in due season we shall reap if we do not lose heart. Galatians 6:9

The road to successful creativity contains bumps, curves, and pit-falls much like the road to any other endeavor that takes practice and effort. Some of the obstacles along the way are a part of the landscape, things we cannot change. Others are the results of our own mistakes or attitudes. To reach our full potential, we must, in a godly manner, deal with the things life throws us. If not, these things will hinder us from truly developing our artistic abilities. Hindrances may come in the form of abandonment by family or friends, a wayward child, the unexpected death of a loved one, the onset of a long-term illness or disability, the sudden loss of income. Each of these things have the power to weaken or paralyze our resolve. Responding in fear or doubt can make the situation worse. God desires trust and expects growth in our lives, even during hardship and struggle. "Be merciful to me, O

God, be merciful to me! For my soul trusts in You; and in the shadow of Your wings I will make my refuge, until these calamities have passed by" (Psalm 57:1).

Learning from adversity, instead of running from it or getting bogged down in self-pity because of it, will teach us how to handle our emotions, as well as our responses, so we can better represent the heart of God. From here, we can use the arts to translate the results of our overcoming into useful messages of hope. Experiences shape our personality. If our only concern is to protect ourselves, our world becomes small and insignificant. When we allow God to protect us, we have wings to soar past pain or disappointment to a productive life that becomes beneficial to those we touch. This chapter deals with the proper handling of things we cannot change and how it can make our creative outlets more effective. It will also show how we can use the arts to keep things in perspective.

Focus and Perspective

I would dare say we've all been hurt to some degree or another and that some have felt more than their fair share of heartache and disappointment. The question I want you to ask yourself is, "How did I respond to being hurt?" I've seen those who not only reacted negatively to situations or toward the ones who offended them, but they also became bitter toward God. A lack of trust controls their emotions and creative activity has all but ceased. If we only consider our pain and loss, we won't recognize God's purpose for allowing these situations to come into our lives. "Many are the afflictions of the righteous, but the LORD delivers him out of them all" (Psalm 34:19). That's if we don't get bitter. "Looking carefully lest anyone fall short of the grace of God; lest any root of bitterness springing up cause trouble, and by this many become defiled" (Hebrews 12:15). Just as incorrect perspective can ruin a painting, so it can ruin a life or many lives if bitterness takes hold.

Trials do not come our way at the surprise of God. He sees all and allows what happens to us. Joseph, the son of Jacob, is an excellent example of a man who encountered hardship yet managed to maintain his integrity through it all. In the beginning of Genesis 37, we find Joseph with everything a person could ever want. He was Dad's favorite son. He wore a coat of many colors, symbolizing a position of honor. He even received dreams from God. Nevertheless, in one fell swoop all that changed as he collided with the fury of his jealous brothers. They stripped him of his coat, threw him into a pit, and planned to kill him. Fearful of what would happen next, he found himself abruptly taken from a safe-haven of wealth and comfort and sold as a slave in Egypt. The life he was accustomed to no longer existed; but God had a plan beyond Joseph's immediate comfort, past what he could see or comprehend at that point. Certainly, the situation changed him, but more importantly, it prepared him for his destiny in God's sovereign plan. It's human nature to look at the present and try to figure things out, but often our success lies in persevering when we don't understand.

Once, while talking with someone about a difficult situation, I jokingly said, "Well you know, we have to live till we die." Then it struck me just how true this statement is. Even if we feel trapped by unfavorable circumstances, we have no other choice but to live through them. How we do this will make or break us and determine our usefulness to God. Joseph was forsaken, not dead. The purposes of God were not complete in his life; therefore, he continued to live and through it all he saw God's promises as "yea and amen." He never lowered his emotional vantage point or changed his perspective to a place where things looked distorted. His focus remained clear and his heart pure toward the Almighty.

The Bible doesn't tell us whether Joseph had any creative ability in the area of traditional arts, but we do know he had a talent for being the best he could be in any given circumstance. Ecclesiastes 9:10 encourages, "Whatever your hand finds to do, do it with your might; for there is no work or device or knowledge or wisdom in the grave where you are going." Joseph's life emulated this verse. For thirteen years, he had to endure a life that wasn't supposed to be his. But wherever he was, whatever he did, it was out of a heart to do his best, even though at times it wasn't fair. When Potiphar's wife falsely accused him because he wouldn't yield to her seductions, his integrity landed him in prison without a chance to defend himself. Psalm 105:18–19 sheds some light on his condition, "They hurt his feet with fetters, he was laid in irons. Until the time that his word came to pass, the word of the LORD tested him." In a state of pain, humiliation, and confusion, he did not lose heart. Instead, he became a model prisoner, willing to help others. He even interpreted dreams for two of them. Nevertheless, his trials continued when he was forgotten about and had to wait for Divine intervention. All in good time though, God brought deliverance and blessed Joseph for having the right attitude. The pain he suffered because of others did not destroy him or cause him to turn his back on God. It did, however, bring maturity to his life and prepared him to rule as second in command over all of Egypt.

"My brethren, count it all joy when you fall into various trials, knowing that the testing of your faith produces patience. But let patience have its perfect work, that you may be perfect and complete, lacking nothing" (James 1:2–4). Through trials, God adjusts our way of thinking, makes us stronger, and better equipped for His service.

Wisdom to Know the Difference

There will be times when circumstances are out of our control, or things we simply cannot change, but how we respond and the actions we take have everything to do with us. If we choose to put our creative outlet aside during tough times, we are putting away a gift that God has given us to make life more manageable. Look at Joni Eareckson Tada. I can only imagine how many times she must have thought something to the effect of, if only I'd been more careful . . . But the diving accident that left her paralyzed from the neck down became an irreversible reality. To help Joni get through the discouragement of her predicament, an occupational therapist gave her a set of pastel pencils and encouraged her to use them. At first, she refused, but then she saw a young man whose physical condition was much worse than her own. He was enthusiastic as he willingly learned to write with a pen between his teeth. This brought conviction to Joni and she began to allow the therapist to teach her how to maneuver the pencils. Through this situation, she found an un-mined talent discovered by circumstance, and though she cannot use her hands, she is an amazing artist; all because she *chose* not to let her physical limitations control her destiny. Her artistic abilities are a direct result of addressing the things she could change. The Prayer of St. Francis of Assisi sums it up best. "God grant me the serenity to accept the things I cannot change, the courage to change the things I can, and the wisdom to know the difference." Accepting God's will, though it may seem harsh at times, is fundamental to our salvation and our witness.

During my teenage years, I wrote poetry; it was my muse and a way to talk to God. The poems were simple and not well written but they filled a void and gave me hope. After I married, poetry was no longer an active part of my life. Thinking about this recently, I realized my thoughts turned to words and rhymes as a teenager because times were tough. My parents were not getting along, our family fell apart and I couldn't do a thing about it. Expressing my innermost thoughts on paper seemed to improve my ability to deal with heartache and frustration.

As we have previously discussed, using creativity is good for our health and emotional well being. But its benefits don't stop here; when put to good use, it's a means to find relief from the storm. Often, one of the first things we dismiss during hardships is our creative outlets. We set them aside in order to deal with our problems, not realizing it could be the very thing God provided to maintain sanity. Plus, this is a double-edged-sword, because we really lose twice if we allow this to happen. First, we forgo the joy and pleasure that comes from being creative and secondly, if we don't take creative action, it can't act as a medicine for the soul. We should also consider that if we no longer birth creative life, we cannot encourage others. Creativity is for all seasons, a truly wonderful gift from God our Father.

If you have read First and Second Samuel, you know that David had more than his share of trials. There were times in his life where things went from bad to worse, but he never lost heart. For example, let's look at his last struggle prior to becoming King of Judah; it is found in 1 Samuel 30. He and his men were returning home after an extended stay in the land of the Philistines. Perhaps they were talking about how nice it would be to see their families again; but as they came over the last ridge, they saw smoke hovering above their village. In utter horror, they made haste to Ziklag and fear gripped their hearts as they wondered if anyone survived. Upon their arrival, they found nothing; all their possessions were gone or destroyed and there was no trace of their wives or children.

Discouragement absorbed each and every thought. They assumed all was lost and sadness overwhelmed them as they "wept until there was no more power to weep" (vs.4). You might think this is as bad as it gets, but 1 Samuel 30:6 goes on to say, "David was greatly distressed; for the people spoke of stoning him." As if this situation was entirely his fault . . . Yet David took heart and "encouraged himself in the Lord" (vs.6). I venture to say his encouragement came in the form of a psalm, like Psalm 34:3–4, "Oh, magnify the LORD with me, and let us exalt His name together. I sought the LORD, and He heard me, and delivered me from all my fears." By strengthening himself through a creative means, David was able to turn the wrath of his men toward a greater cause. With faith restored, they sought God, received the battle plan, pursued the enemy and recovered all (1 Samuel 30:19). Within three days of these events, David became King of Judah and his previously discouraged men were exalted with him. God used what looked to be a disaster as an occasion for blessing—by defeating and spoiling the enemy, David had the means to send gifts to all those who helped him gain the throne, thus securing his kingdom.

Could you imagine what would have happened if David's men chose to remain dejected or if they went ahead and stoned him? When situations come to dampen our spirits or cause us fear, we need to trust God knows all and has a plan beyond our present needs. Using creative outlets in a positive way helps us to manage our emotions and maintain a godly point of view.

Many of David's Psalms start with a cry for help or in a tone of discouragement, but they always end with hope and a thankful heart that God is in control. "But I will sing of Your power; yes, I will sing aloud of Your mercy in the morning; for You have been my defense and refuge in the day of my trouble" (Psalm 59:16).

In Psalm 137:1–4 we find a different response, though:

By the rivers of Babylon, there we sat down, yea, we wept when we remembered Zion. We hung our harps upon the willows in the midst of it. For there those who carried us away captive asked of us a song, and those who plundered us requested mirth, saying, 'Sing us one of the songs of Zion!' How shall we sing the LORD's song in a foreign land?

Here we have a group of Israelites taken captive in the land of Babylon. These people were discouraged, just as David and his men were when they came to Ziklag. The difference lay in their heart attitude and was manifested by the way they handled their trial. They did not accept what they could not change and refused to *encourage themselves in the Lord.* They chose to feel sorry for themselves, preferring to hang their *harps upon the willows,* rather than singing a song of praise to God in the presence of their enemies. They willingly hung up their creative opportunity. They let the situation get the best of them instead of making the best of the situation. Their harps were not taken from them; they freely set them aside. Their captors even asked of them a song, encouraging them to use their creative outlets, but they rejected the offer.

Now, you could say the enemy was mocking them by asking for a song, but in reality, it was an opportunity to rise above the pain and sorrow to find hope again. Words have power and their words were negative. They should have seized the moment, grabbed their harps and lifted a song of praise to God. By doing so, it would have brought emotional freedom though their chains remained.

Most of us could say we've felt captive by circumstances at one time or another, held prisoner by things beyond our control. The lesson to learn, just as Joni learned, is not to become captive in our hearts and minds. If we are not careful, we will fall into the same trap of hanging up our artistic endeavors and our heart of worship. Don't put aside the very thing that will help bring you to the throne of God, where He becomes the "help of your countenance" (Psalm 42:5). Psalm 108:2–3 says, "Awake, flute and harp! I will awaken the dawn. I will praise You, O LORD, among the peoples, and I will sing praises to You among the nations." There will be times when we have to shake ourselves and push our creative outlet into action. God gave us talents as gifts, not to neglect, but to use. He knew these gifts would benefit us far beyond the temporal pleasure we get from doing artwork when things are going well.

Not long ago, a local high school student died in a car accident. The funeral was held at our church and Lisa was asked to sing two songs. Grieved by the premature death, and a very emotional person as it is, Lisa knew it would be hard to sing without crying. But then to add to her sorrow, just as she was ready to leave for service, the phone rang. It was her doctor calling about the possibility of uterine cancer and an appointment was set up for further testing. Keep in mind, she was to sing in less than an hour. I knew nothing of the call or of her fear of cancer until later that week and I was amazed by how Lisa held her composure and sang with such grace and beauty. Beyond her creative outlet ministering to the four hundred grieving people at the funeral, it caused faith to arise in her own heart for her own situation.

I have also learned this lesson through personal experience. For years I lived with constant pain and fatigue, a condition known as fibromyalgia. On numerous occasions, I felt overwhelmed. To ward off impending depression, I would quilt, paint, or write. These creative outlets helped get my mind off the pain and improved my ability to fight the good fight of faith, knowing that God does all things well. The result of my actions brought emotional comfort and I usually felt better physically. I did not hang *up my harp* when things got tough, even though at times that was exactly what I *felt* like doing. I'm not suggesting it's easy, but I do know it's worth it.

Hast Thou Considered My Servant Job?

In the first chapter of Job, we discover he had some trials of his own . . . like losing all that he had, including his ten children in one day. How devastating, as servants came one after another carrying the news of loss and destruction. These circumstances were clearly outside Job's control, but where do we find him in this dark hour? On his face before God—worshipping. We know David was the great psalmist. He could play the harp with skill and was musically inclined. But the Bible doesn't tell us if Job had any musical talents or if he could even carry a tune. It didn't matter, what did matter was that he used the creative means of worship to come before God in a time of need and there he found comfort (Job 1:20).

We also see through this experience that Job had a flare for the poetic as he wrote, "Naked I came from my mother's womb, and naked shall I return there. The LORD gave, and the LORD has taken away; blessed be the name of the LORD" (Job 1:21). Creative means helped him through this time of loss. He may not have understood why these things happened, but he trusted the Almighty and proved it by his actions.

Job's wife lost everything in one day too! She was bereaved of her children just as Job was, but we do not hear any thing about how she handled the situation. Some time later though, in Chapter 2, Job is struck with boils from head to foot. Watching her husband suffer in extreme pain, especially after all they had previously lost, was more than she could bear. This time she speaks, "Do you still hold fast to your integrity? Curse God and die!" (Job 2:9). No song, no poem, no heart of worship came from Job's wife. Instead, she became very bitter and even hateful toward God. Thankfully, Job did not take heed to her request and in time God blessed him with more than he had in the first place (Job 42). If he had listened to the broken heart of his wife, he would have missed the blessing—and so would she.

Trials are a part of life. We can't see the end from the beginning nor understand why God allows certain things to happen; but through it all, He longs for us to trust Him and maintain our integrity. Better times are ahead of every difficulty—if we keep our eyes on the prize and don't give up in the season of testing.

Remember, God has given us creative outlets to help us come to Him in every situation with a heart of worship and thanksgiving. When we handle hard times in a godly manner, it makes us stronger and our creative abilities will grow right along with us, if we don't set them aside. Utilizing our God-given talents in the face of adversity is not only our privilege, but a wise choice.

Helping Others through Their Pain

The heart may lack a song in a difficult season, but thank God for the people who give us songs when we don't have one of our own. Some of the most touching hymns were written during hardships. H.G. Spafford wrote "It Is Well With My Soul" after his four daughters were killed in a shipwreck off the coast of New Foundland. This song exemplifies Spafford's determination to focus on his Savior and not on his loss. Even though the accident was dreadful, his ability to pen these words brought comfort and hope; creative expression helped ease his pain.

This song is still sung today, and a perfect illustration of how using creative outlets can strengthen others while facing their own difficulties. Sometimes just knowing that others have also gone through similar situations and overcome may provide us courage to do the same. 2 Corinthians 1:3–4 says it best,

> *Blessed be the God and Father of our Lord Jesus Christ, the*
> *Father of mercies and God of all comfort, who comforts us in*
> *all our tribulation, that we may be able to comfort those who*

*are in any trouble, with the comfort with which we ourselves
are comforted by God.*

Our growth through trials and the ability to translate that growth into a viable creative expression, no matter what the form, can bring comfort and encouragement to others.

Another noteworthy example is Francis Scott Key, who wrote "The Star Spangled Banner" while a prisoner on a British warship. From the porthole of his confinement, he could see the American flag proudly waving over the fort. This not only gladdened his heart, it bolstered a sense of pride for his countrymen who would not back down under the full furry of enemy fire. Grabbing pen and parchment, he wrote words of jubilant determination, which have become our National Anthem. We proudly sing these words today, all because of a man who used a creative outlet in a time of adversity. These songwriters and poets, along with countless others, used creativity to deal with hard realities and encouraged themselves to make it through. How empty the heart, how cold the world, if no creative expression was birthed out of other's pain, teaching us to sing through our own. Artists, throughout the ages, have left us a creative history to use and enjoy. May we continue the legacy of hope by passing the fruit of our talents on to the next generation.

We can all use singing and worship as a form of encouragement. Ephesians 5:17–20 tells us,

> *Therefore do not be unwise, but understand what the will of the Lord is. And do not be drunk with wine, in which is dissipation; but be filled with the Spirit, speaking to one another in psalms and hymns and spiritual songs, singing and making melody in your heart to the Lord, giving thanks always for all things to God the Father in the name of our Lord Jesus Christ.*

Music or singing may not even be your form of creativity, but it's something we can all use to keep a thankful attitude toward God in good times and bad. Psalm 32:7 tells us, "You are my hiding place; You shall preserve me from trouble; You shall surround me with songs of deliverance. Selah." Look God's way, He'll provide the song. And don't use the excuse, "I can't sing . . ." because Psalm 95:2 clearly states, "Let us come before His presence with thanksgiving; let us shout joyfully to Him with psalms." It is not a matter of skill, but rather a matter of the heart. When our voice is lifted in sincerity, God gladly listens.

In Acts 16, we find Paul and Silas beaten and thrown into prison. You have probably already guessed what they were doing . . . that's right, singing! God heard their worship and set them free; which in turn brought revival to that region. If they had put the art of song away in the midnight hour, they probably would have found themselves still in prison come morning light.

The emphasis of this chapter has dealt with not putting creativity aside during times of trials. Sing unto God a new song and see Him move on your behalf. The change may be external and the situation resolved or it may only be an internal strengthening of the soul. Either way, a song and a heart of worship will loose the prison bars from your mind and hope can triumph.

Though we have focused on music and song, these are not the only expressions helpful in rising above difficulties. Many other forms of creativity work just as well to lift our thoughts off the problems and unto God. Some find scrapbooking or quilting to be very relaxing and comforting, for others, it's splashing paint on a canvas or keeping a journal. In the summer, gardening is good therapy. What is your muse? Does it turn your focus to God? Does it bring you closer to Him?

The enemy of our souls wants to bring discouragement by weakening our confidence in God. If he can do so, it will hinder our witness for the Lord; that's why the devil said to God, and I paraphrase, "Job is only serving you because he is blessed, take the blessings away and he will curse you" (Job1:10–11). Job proved the devil wrong and so should we when adversity comes our way. Romans 8:28 encourages, "And we know that all things work together for good to those who love God, to those who are the called according to His purpose." Let's believe God's word is true and trust in His sovereign plan for our lives. Determine to maintain a pure heart of worship, even if you don't understand (at the moment) what good can come of a bad situation.

chapter fourteen

things we bring upon ourselves

That you may be sons of your Father in heaven; for He makes His sun rise on the evil and on the good, and sends rain on the just and on the unjust. Matthew 5:45

All God's purposes go beyond us, even if the initial work is personal. He uses tough situations in our lives to accomplish things that wouldn't come about if everything were running smoothly. For example, can you imagine the outcome if the Apostle Paul never went to prison or spent time under house arrest? He might not have penned those letters to the churches, which in turn became a large portion of the New Testament. This demonstrates how his creative outlet proved vital to him during his time of need, and to all those who would be encouraged by the content of his writings, even to this day. At the time though, he may well have thought he could accomplish a great deal more if he were out preaching; but God's plan was bigger and went farther than Paul's immediate comfort or ministry. What looked like a hindrance to him became a blessing to every generation that followed. His epistles are still used to preach the Gospel of Jesus Christ today. Once we accept the fact that hindrances and hardships carry purpose beyond ourselves, our mind-set will improve and our service for the Lord will take on greater meaning.

In my own life, God used a lack of health to bring me to a place where I was willing to write. Before I had fibromyalgia, I was strong; I liked physical activity and was convinced there were better things to do with my time than sit at a computer. God however, had a different plan for my life and it took this illness to adjust my way of thinking. The pain and fatigue slowed my pace to the point where I understood and appreciated the need for creative outlets. Here again, the purpose went beyond me—to you.

Our talents cannot bless others if we do not use them. Some time ago my brother, Paul, gave me an old shoebox filled with several well-written poems. "What a waste," I thought as I read those passionate and descriptive words. They were powerful and ought to be shared with others. Therefore, I suggested he organize his poems and asked how long it would take to write a few more so that he would have enough for his very own book of poetry. The thought of publication sparked fresh enthusiasm in Paul and he began writing again. Within a few days of our conversation, he called me with a new poem and it wasn't many days later when the phone rang again . . . another poem. He even talked of having his older poems critiqued, edited, and made ready for print. Things were moving steadily forward; he even decided upon a name for the book and came up with an idea for the layout.

Then abruptly the phone stopped ringing. Weeks went by without a word. Concerned at the sudden lack of communication, I gave Paul a call and inquired after his health and well-being. On the other end of the line was a depressed voice, dejected by personal difficulties. After a time of trying to bring hope and godly encouragement, I asked how his poetry was coming along. I thought this might lift his spirits and help get his mind on something constructive. His response grieved me. "I can't write," he snapped. "I don't have the heart for it. And anyway, how am I supposed to write when I feel like this?"

Do you see what happened? Paul set his creative aspirations aside because of personal problems. My objective changed from encouragement to a challenge. "Pick up your pen and write," I admonished. "Pour out your heart and let poetic melody bring comfort. Not only for yourself, but for all those who need to know they are not alone in their own trials."

I was pleased when a few days later the phone rang and Paul had written a new poem, a poem filled with faith. I could hear a difference not only in his words but also in the tone of his voice. Taking creative action brightened his day and helped put things back into perspective. Here is the poem by Paul Howard.

The Song of the Song Sparrow

The song sparrow did sing,
In the cold misty rain,
As I trudged along stacking wood.
Sparing little she sang,
And called from time to time,
Longing with songs and rhymes,
The rain soon slowed and stopped.
The sun started to shine,
And the song of the song sparrow,
With flick of beak and neck,
Continued heartily to grow.
But why she sang, I could not see.
And yet her songs still come
These many years later.
A simple truth is all she speaks,
"Not one sparrow shall fall
Without the Father's will."
While times of trudging must need come,
Along with other storms,

The sparrow's song of mirth
Tells how much more this life is worth.

This poem is a perfect illustration of the constructive effect creative outlets can have on our moods. Yet, creativity alone is not a fix-all. It cannot replace time spent in prayer, reading the Bible, going to Church, and fellowshipping with other Christians. These are all needful to strengthen our walk with God and to maintain health, wholeness, and godly attitudes. However, utilizing God's gifts can help bring hope and healing to our lives when discouragement looms.

As you finish reading the words of this next poem, stop and ask yourself how it made you feel.

Can the heart feel pain and woe
Amidst a stormy night
Only to find when morning comes
There is a lack of light
Through the veil of tears no sun has shown
For in the night the pain has grown
Blinding the hope that comes with morning

Did you feel saddened by this negative predicament? Creative outlets can leave us discouraged or even add to our disappointments if they don't lead us to our Creator. The second part of Psalm 30:5 tells us, "Weeping may endure for a night, but joy comes in the morning." Using our talents won't necessarily change the situation, but they can help strengthen us emotionally. It's not wrong to add negative sentiments to our outlet as long as we don't get stuck there. This poem would improve with another stanza ending on a positive note.

Morgan battles a life-threatening illness and despair often grips her heart. Recently she told me she felt like she was drowning, but she went on to say her journal entry for that day changed her outlook. She described her mood in the form of an allegory, starting with a character caught in the quagmire of doom, but as she wrote, her focus turned to Jesus and her words turned to hope. Emotionally she felt better—though her sickness remained.

An Analogy

Most of us behave favorably when things are going well, so with that thought in mind, let's consider the weather for a moment. If we could always have it our way, we would wake to a glorious sunrise, followed by a day filled with beautiful blue skies and end with breathtaking sunsets. No storms, no rain, life would be great, creativity would flourish and all would be well with the world—right? Not exactly. It wouldn't take long before we stopped appreciating perfect days and, even worse, we would die for the lack of rain.

Thankfully, God knows best and is faithful to give us what we need, not just what we want. If this is true in the natural realm, why do we automatically think God's upset with us when the "weather" of our lives becomes stormy? Even the most upright person goes through tough times. "Have you considered My servant Job . . ." (Job 1:8)— and every other person mentioned in the Bible . . . They all weathered difficulties and endured temptations. Trials are a part of life.

Art of distinction requires mood and contrast, something to cause the eye to linger. The same is true with a novel. While it must have purpose and direction, it also requires conflict to make it a success. What brings us to creative greatness is no different from the ingredients needed for the art itself. Personal conflict often becomes the reason we produce art. If everything is always roses and sunshine, creative drought is inevitable, ideas become ordinary or weak and nothing produces the vibrant results we desire. Refreshing rains, and even occasional storms, can rejuvenate creative flow, bringing with them new life and often a new course of action.

The fact of the matter is, trials bring about feelings and responses we don't have when things are running smoothly. Therefore, we must learn to take those feelings and work toward a positive outcome to our problems. Through prayer, Jesus can show us what He wants to accomplish. It may be as simple as a heart of worship, or He could be calling us to a creative expression that will help others find their way to Him. There is always a purpose, even in times of pruning, which ultimately brings forth a greater harvest.

Hindrances We Bring on Ourselves

This next section deals with things we *can* change, overcome, or remove from our lives. One of the biggest hindrances to successful creativity is looking for approval from others. To impress people, especially those held in esteem, brings great satisfaction and why shouldn't it? I've even heard artists say they measure their ability by how well they do in juried art shows. Praise promotes confidence and rightly so, but what if the all-important compliment never comes? Or even worse, what if those who examine your art have an unfavorable opinion? What happens then? For many young artists, it throws a great shadow of doubt over their creative ability. Those affected by the need for approval often resort to protecting their tender souls by hiding their talent. Though an innate desire yearns for liberty, the lack of affirmation holds many a heart captive. Small private attempts may ensue, but true freedom of expression will not exist until the assurance that comes from God becomes stronger than the judgments of those held in regard.

Why do we allow others to have such sway over our lives? Why do we gauge our worth and even our fulfillment by their opinions? Many miss the creative experience because of intimidation and as long as this mindset prevails, it negates God's purpose for the arts. Regret also has a way of catching up with those who don't use their creative outlets, especially as maturity and confidence increase through experience. Thoughts of what might have been if the opinion of others had only been different. It's not too late; the creative journey does not come with a deadline, yet it can only begin by taking action.

Pressures to Perform

Sometimes we can't avoid outside pressures to perform. Therefore, we must learn to deal with them. Once while teaching a watercolor class, I noticed a woman in tears. Concerned, I inquired of the problem. "My husband will laugh at this," she cried. "It's so bad!" Do you see how apprehension of her husband's response overshadowed her ability to succeed? He expected excellence . . . she needed approval . . . both, without allowing adequate time for improvement. These attitudes cause unnecessary damage and usually bring with them a lack of determination to master anything. Unfortunately, this is not an isolated case.

This woman's quandary gave me an opportunity to reiterate to my class the concept that each attempt is a stepping-stone to success. Some steps may seem small or insignificant, but as long as we keep moving forward, goals are achievable. The key is to keep our ambitions attainable, especially at the beginning. Once accomplished, new loftier goals can be set.

I encountered a similar occurrence near the beginning of writing this book. All was going well until I started transferring my notes into the computer. Suddenly, I realized my dream could become a reality and I panicked. "Oh no," I thought. "What if it's not good enough?" Doubts concerning my ability obscured the reason for developing these concepts in the first place and I became fearful of the outcome. Would people like it? Could I really motivate others to use their talents?

These and many other such thoughts almost caused me to quit. Thankfully, God intervened and showed me I was not the only one with nervous apprehensions. And yes, dealing with subjects such as this would encourage people to create and assist them in conquering personal insecurities. Ironically, my first editor gave me a very honest and accurate evaluation of my efforts, telling me that writing was probably a good outlet for me on a personal level, but it did not seem suitable for publication. Fortunately, I had matured to the point where rejection no longer controlled my life and I realized the need for approval had nothing to do with it. This was not a death sentence; I simply had to face the reality that major improvements were necessary and I must work at achieving them. So I continued to write, starting as poorly as my first stroke of paint; but line upon line and a million changes later, there is hope. The process taught me perseverance; the result of using this creative outlet, despite a shaky beginning, has brought lasting fulfillment. We will all encounter difficulties along this creative journey, but when met with determination, we not only become stronger artists, we become stronger people.

Need for approval hinders the onset of all kinds of activities, even when desire is present. Some never put paint on a canvas or take a ballroom dance class. The woodworking shop remains empty and the quilting material is never purchased. Pen and paper stay in the drawer and the instrument resides in its case. While these things may seem insignificant, the underlying attitude controls other areas of our lives as well, such as avoiding career choices and allowing aspirations to melt away. We must conquer the fears that keep us from experiencing life to the fullest and one of the quickest ways to do so is to stop worrying about what everyone else will think.

It's good to want to do things well; it's even okay to want acceptance and approval from others, as long as it doesn't become the consuming factor. Fear of failure or rejection often immobilizes us, which is exactly what the devil wants. This fear keeps us from using our talents for God and His kingdom.

Are You a Perfectionist?

Many are stuck in the *have to do it perfect* mode. This affects some people's willingness to try creative outlets. For others, it prevents them from fully developing their talents because they couldn't master the process quickly enough. Then there are those consumed by the need to achieve. They strive long and hard to reach their goals and often succeed, but it takes its toll both physically and mentally, leaving no time for art, and many other things, for that matter. All these things can hinder and even stop the creative process.

If you're a perfectionist, ask yourself why. Did your parents demand perfection? Is it so you can feel better about yourself? Do you want to impress those around you and receive praise? Are you critical of other's best or jealous of those who surpass you? Do you simply like quality work? Is Jesus in the equation? I realize these are hard questions, but when we are honest about the whys, God can adjust our wrong motives and use our positive ones for His service.

Matthew 5:48 says, "Therefore you shall be perfect, just as your Father in heaven is perfect." Hebrews 13:20–21 concludes with a prayer, "Now may the God of peace . . . make you complete in every good work to do His will, working in you what is well pleasing in His sight, through Jesus Christ, to whom be glory forever and ever. Amen." God desires perfection, but He knows it's only possible through Him. Our incentive has to be about doing our best for Jesus, not for our own glory or recognition. Colossians 3:23 puts things in perspective, "And whatever you do, do it heartily, as to the Lord and not to men." At times, we lose sight of this verse and try to promote our own worth or flaunt our own abilities.

For those of us who are perfectionists, we need to examine our hearts to see what drives us. A godly desire for perfection leaves room for failure or coming short of our lofty goals. It is here we find mercy and grace cheering us on to try again. A selfish desire for perfection leads to sulking, struggles, or self-hatred when perfection is not attained. These attitudes can interfere with our ability to proceed and often leave us unwilling to move constructively forward. However, just because we can't master certain areas, doesn't mean we don't have talent in others.

On the other hand, when successes do come, does pride take the lead? Remember, "Every good gift and every perfect gift is from above, and comes down from the Father of lights . . ."(James 1:17). The motivation of our heart determines true success. Let's use our talents with God in mind; it's only by His good and perfect gifts that we have the ability to create in the first place. Our ultimate goal should be to further His kingdom and to bless others.

In reference to Lessons in the Sand, found in Chapter Two, the waves of the ocean not only wash away the poorly constructed sand sculptures, but in the end, even the best or *perfect* fall. There is no lasting worth in perfection unless it accomplishes something of eternal value.

This book forced me to deal with my own need for approval. In my early drafts, I applied "God points" to my "motivational book about creativity." Then I hesitated long enough to wonder: if I use a Christian premise, would it sell? Maybe I should just focus on the arts, this way I could "reach a broader range of people." Turning to prayer for direction, a scripture dropped into my heart, "For what will it profit a man if he gains the whole world, and loses his own soul" (Mark 8:36)? This verse helped me realize that my success wasn't about getting published or the amount of books I sold. If my purpose didn't bring glory to my Maker, it would have no eternal value—even if some thought it a winner. Jesus called me to promote the arts in the light of His word and to convey the importance of using creativity to preach the gospel. I felt it better to hear "well done" from the clouds of heaven than from the crowds of men.

Other Problems with Perfection

In the sport of baseball, very seldom does a pitcher throw a *perfect* game. If he does, accolades fly . . . until the next game. Glory is short lived and expectations are high. Perfection demands perfection; but we are imperfect people, living in an imperfect world. Pressure to live at unrealistic levels of performance is often destructive, as well as unnecessary. A pitcher doesn't need to throw a perfect game to win.

Recently, a painting of mine received the Most Popular vote at an Art Show. Was I excited? You bet. Then it hit me, what if I don't do well in the next show? Can I maintain that level of expectation? Reality check—it doesn't matter. Even if my art is over-looked at the next show, it won't make me any less of an artist. If I do my best, I must be content, award or not. Don't get me wrong, I love awards and approval, who doesn't? But we cannot base our success solely upon them.

There is nothing wrong with wanting to do a thing well, even perfectly, unless it hinders us from doing anything at all. Our happiness should never be dependent upon recognition from our accomplishments, especially when the praise of others is hard to find, fleeting as the wind, and as fickle as the masses.

Art is Subjective

Who is to say what's "perfect" anyway? Art is subjective. Not everyone will see things the same way we do. What appeals to you may not appeal to me or vice-versa.

Art has rules, concepts to learn, and basic disciplines to master. We can improve our skills by taking classes, using self-help materials, and practicing. When we are pleased with the results of our creative outlet, many will enjoy and appreciate our efforts, but there will always be those who won't be impressed. Differences of opinion and a variety of tastes are a fact of life; the secret is allowing for individuality without being threatened by it. As artists, we need to be confident in our own unique style and not so quickly disappointed if our work doesn't appeal to everyone. We should never allow others to decide our worth, especially when based merely upon an opinion.

I find juried art shows interesting because what wins often has to do with the judges' personal preferences. In one show, realistic landscapes may fair well and in the next show, modern styles take top honors. Different judges, different personalities, different winners. Sometimes those who are serious about winning even try to find out what the judges like and create accordingly. I've entered artwork that didn't impress the judges and honestly, it wasn't good enough to win; but with other pieces I've submitted, I thought they deserved better placement. The bottom line: art is subjective and not everyone will see it our way, nor can everyone place at the top.

I can be quite opinionated when it comes to the arts—all based upon my own likes, of course. I love going to art shows, galleries, and museums, to see what's out there and glean inspiration from other artists. I usually go with family or friends and we enjoy taking our time and analyzing each piece. We talk about the different drawings, paintings, and sculptures—each of us like or dislike different ones for different reasons. The judges have their own observations of what deserves top honors and why. Likewise, when the public votes for their favorite, there are always a variety of choices for the same diversity of reasons. Art is subjective.

Many years ago, my mom enjoyed painting, but gave it up to raise six kids and work on the family farm. When the time of leisure came in her life, health problems hindered her creative homecoming. Finally, her strength returned and I again encouraged her to paint. All was going well and it seemed as if the paints would be out of the box any day. But then she started looking at the artwork hung around my house. "I might as well not even try, I could never do this good," she said in a disheartened tone. Consequently, her paints remain in the old box that has stored them for years.

It's amazing what will keep us from enjoying creative outlets and it's unfortunate how many people allow outside influences to shipwreck their creative voyage. To amplify the problem, many discourage themselves without anyone else ever saying a word. The artists that did the paintings my mom felt inferior to never told her she wasn't good enough or that she shouldn't bother. No, these were her own qualms, which kept her from creative fulfillment. How often do our thoughts become our own worst enemy? There are enough obstacles in life without needlessly adding to them.

chapter fifteen

overcoming adversity

*We are hard-pressed on every side, yet not crushed; we are
perplexed, but not in despair; persecuted, but not forsaken;
struck down, but not destroyed—2Corinthians 4:8–9*

Winter gave way to spring and it was time to tap the Maple trees.
For a home schooling project, I took my children to a nearby grove
where we helped friends gather sap and learned how to make maple
syrup. While there, I noticed a tree with a very odd shape. Nothing
was unusual about its broad base, but about twelve feet up, the main
body of the tree took a sharp turn and grew sideways like the branches
of a mighty oak. Then within six or seven feet, it took another sharp
turn back toward heaven, growing tall and strong like the other trees.
This seemed peculiar, so I walked over to get a closer look, and realized lightning had caused the deformity. I find it interesting that even
though the imposing jolt caused damage, it did not destroy the tree's
purpose or potential. By sheer determination to live, it endured cir-

cumstances outside its control and grew to maturity. Life will deal us our share of blows too, but when handled properly they build character and make us stronger, both internally and externally.

Another reason this tree caught my attention was because the *scars* were only noticeable if you looked closely. How often do we visibly wear our scars as constant reminders of personal anguish or self-pity? These attitudes do not represent the heart of God, nor do they bring Him glory. He may allow situations to come to teach us or to change our ways, but never exclusively for the sake of hurt—even though some difficulties do cause pain. Nor should we feel justified in expecting sympathy from others. Life continues and we must choose to carry on the best we can without making it obvious to everyone. This reminds me of Matthew 6:16 where it says, "Moreover, when you fast, do not be like the hypocrites, with a sad countenance. For they disfigure their faces that they may appear to men to be fasting. Assuredly, I say to you, they have their reward." God knows what we're going through, that should be comfort and hope enough, especially when He is faithful to reward on an eternal scale.

Have you ever experienced a blow that tried to kill your creative desire or weaken your commitment to participate? Did you consider it an opportunity to stand tall through the storm? Are you the kind of person who allows for setbacks, determined to rise above even the unexpected? Some people grow stronger, while others get bitter or feel like quitting when critical comments come. A vast range of responses are possible, but there are those who make things worse with the, "Fine, I just won't try anymore" attitude. This affects more than art. We can't just quit every time something becomes hard or because others challenge us to do better. Anything worth having should be worth working for, even fighting for, just as the tree that fought to survive and succeeded.

Life is far too short to waste time feeling sorry for ourselves. Sometimes it takes tenacity, like that of a prizefighter: he might get knocked down, but if he's not out, he still has the opportunity to get up and land a punch that will silence his opponent. Storms may try to beat us down, but as we purpose to pull through, we should be mindful of God's faithfulness and grateful for His provision in our lives. With His help, we can overcome adversity, while improving creative ability. Trials often incite thoughts or emotions that normally don't occur when everything is going fine. A sensitive heart can find hope through producing constructive art in a time of need.

Going back to the maple tree for a moment, as lightning struck and split the trunk, the immediate damage must have been obvious and the tree's appearance uncomely. Making a practical comparison, there will be times when our creative efforts won't look or sound so great, either. However, if we are hit with the truth and someone points out a weakness, do we whither up and die or do we rise to the occasion and work harder? Does it become a hindrance or a help? The answer lies with our perception.

Criticism comes in two forms: constructive and destructive. The major difference between the two should be understood before encountering critiques of our creative endeavors. Constructive criticism, when received, helps us work toward mastering techniques and artistic success. Destructive criticism only has the power to injure our resolve—if we allow it to be so.

Constructive Criticism

Criticism given with the idea of urging improvement is *not* comparable to a bolt of lightning, though it may seem like it at times. A more appropriate word in this case would be *critique*; a pointing out of flaws, so when repaired, the piece becomes structurally sound and more enjoyable to view, to hear, to read, etc. When we have a teachable attitude, we see storms as a means to bring the refreshing rain needed for growth. What is often taken for *winds of adversity* are no more than the breezes of correction meant for our benefit. Constructive criticism becomes advantageous once we learn to get past the initial disappointment. For example, it has become a tradition for me to ask my husband, Ron, what he thinks of my paintings, either just before I'm finished or if I'm having trouble with a piece. It never fails, he always notices every mistake and has an answer for ameliorating each problem. I appreciate his advice when I'm *not* pleased with an area, but it's hard to take when I think a painting is complete and I'm looking for a compliment. Nevertheless, once I see his point, I'll fix the problem and the finished piece is always better. Yet, there have been times of real frustration, especially when it was hard to change or mend a weak spot to the point of meeting with Ron's approval and then I get upset. His response, "Well, Hon, then don't ask for my opinion, I'm only trying to help." So back to the studio I go, knowing this momentary aggravation will make the final piece of art worth the effort if I persist. Ron's advice has enhanced and even saved many a painting and I am thankful he loves me enough to be honest; his critiques have made me a better artist.

Often friends or family members will tell us our work is great, or we sing beautifully, because they don't want to hurt our feelings. Yet, a polite compliment can be just as destructive as a sharp word, if not given in truth. It may seem good to our ego, but it hinders real progress.

During one of my watercolor classes, Roxanne thanked me for giving an honest evaluation of her artwork. Everyone else she had shown her paintings to said how "terrific they were." Actually, they were quite good for how long she had been painting, but there were noticeable weaknesses in each piece. She knew this too, but couldn't identify the problem, so I pointed out how her art lacked contrast. Roxanne struggled with making the dark areas dark enough because she preferred a softer pastel look. She needed to step out of her comfort zone and deepen the shadows. By the fourth lesson, she had a good grasp of the concept and was well on her way to honest praise.

Another time I was talking with Roger about a book he had just written and how he was in the process of finding a publisher. Because I was in the middle of writing my own book, I asked several questions, including one about the plot. After listening for a while, I asked if he had any conflict in the story. "Oh, yes." he said with enthusiasm, "I put that at the end," then proceeded to explain it. Now I had just met Roger and wasn't sure if he would willingly accept advice; therefore, I asked if I could give him a suggestion. He consented and I encouraged him to find a way to move the conflict up a few chapters. I feared his readers would not find the book interesting enough because his conflict was so close to the end.

This could have been a disappointing blow; a strike of lightening to Roger, seeing his book was already complete. Though he looked surprised by my comment, he replied, "I belong to a writers group and none of the others writers ever told me where I could improve my work, instead, they always said how good it was." Human nature compels us to welcome praise, but it might not be the best way to accomplish our goals. Roger expected constructive criticism from his peers, but never found it. I, on the other hand, believed it more advantageous for Roger to hear truth than to receive accolades from a few and never get published.

It's not always easy, though. I remember when Stephanie first started editing this book. It lacked ease and continuity, sentences were choppy and often unclear; which required drastic revisions. However, she didn't make all the changes herself; she showed me where improvements were necessary and taught me to write better. At times, it was overwhelming and publication seemed impossible. Yet, because of my commitment to this project and her willingness to honestly confront the weak sections, we made it to print. Enduring constructive criticism with a good attitude will cause us to grow as people, as well as artists, and make us better equipped to reach our desired destination. I don't know anyone who enjoys hearing what his/her weaknesses are, but success is possible for those who are willing to learn, practice, and persevere.

Destructive Criticism

Think about the following verse before reading this section. "If you faint in the day of adversity, your strength is small" (Proverbs 24:10).

If criticism comes in a destructive manner, don't faint. Consider who made the comment and why. The person could be envious of your ability or success. Perhaps they think negative remarks will make you feel inferior, whereby manipulating your response and hindering your confidence. Weakened self-assurance can inhibit one's willingness to go public with their talents. If the pressure is too great or the hurt too deep, you may forgo the next talent contest or art show. Stop for a moment and ask yourself how you respond to cutting words; consider whether they have deterred you from your creative outlet. Jealousy exists because of our fallen nature and jealous people try to do away with competition so they appear better. Don't be taken aback when it happens; many control their fortunes by a cut-throat mentality with no moral conscience or conviction. You cannot let a sharp jolt of cruelty influence your destiny. Stand strong against the winds of adversity, and create!

Bear in mind, some people aren't jealous or guilty of ill intentions; they just never have an encouraging word to say to anyone. Learn to discern whether criticism is legitimate and act appropriately.

Have you ever been struck by the lightning of rude or inconsiderate words? It hurts and can be detrimental if not handled correctly. Paula told me recently how she found comfort in writing poetry when she was younger, but a few *Christian* friends were quite critical of the things she wrote before she was saved. They told her the poems were evil and should be thrown out. Because Paula had such a passion for the Lord and wanted to please Him, she not only threw away the poetry, she quit writing all together. What makes this story even worse, these comments were made over twenty years ago. A God-given talent was buried because of *well-meaning,* yet, *ill-advised* words spoken to a newborn Christian. It is unfortunate that Luke 17:2 didn't come to mind on this occasion for it says, "It would be better for him if a millstone were hung around his neck, and he were thrown into the sea, than that he should offend one of these little ones." If poetry helped Paula cope with life before she gave her heart to Jesus, how much more could she have used this gift for His glory as she matured in her knowledge of Him? She needed guidance—not a death sentence to her creative outlet.

Now is the time for Paula, and all of you in similar situations, to leave behind the destructive blows of the past and begin the creative journey anew. God is looking for increase from the talents He has given. Excuses leave us empty and disappointed. Actions make us useful in the Kingdom of God.

Something worth mentioning about the tree struck by lightening—it still produces sap for maple syrup and we enjoy the sweet result of its overcoming. If you've been wounded or discouraged, purpose in your heart to press through. Strengthen your creative muscles by exercising your talents. Demonstrate your commitment to persevering by placing your work in the next art exhibition or participating in an upcoming talent show. Prize or no prize, you win because you've triumphed over the blow of destructive criticism.

Condemnation

Living with condemnation is another reason people have a tendency to shy away from creative things. The past is one of the biggest enemies of our future. Often, creative activity doesn't find its way to fruition because it's stuffed beneath pain and failure.

> *The elders have ceased gathering at the gate, and the young men from their music. The joy of our heart has ceased; our dance has turned into mourning. The crown has fallen from our head. Woe to us, for we have sinned! Because of this our heart is faint; because of these things our eyes grow dim.* (Lamentations 5:14–17)

This verse clearly shows wholesome creativity stops when sin is present. Direction becomes unclear. Vitality and usefulness are gone. But 2 Chronicles 7:14 admonishes, "If My people who are called by My name will humble themselves, and pray and seek My face, and turn from their wicked ways, then I will hear from heaven, and will forgive their sin and heal their land." Beloved, there is forgiveness and a fresh start with God.

Generally, people who live in guilt or condemnation abstain from anything that involves healthy pleasure. To inflict pain by the denial of a fulfilling hobby or enjoyable activity makes them believe they are appeasing God. Being creative is fun, and to have fun is unacceptable to the condemned soul. This kind of thinking traps the individual in a perpetual cycle of diminishing self-worth, overshadowing hope and keeping them from the source of help. Their heads hang down and nothing seems worthwhile. This feeling also keeps the mind consumed with thinking of ways to become more *worthy* of God's love. Self-condemnation prevents people from accepting the power of the cross and the forgiveness that comes through true repentance. Deadworks or feeling sorry for ourselves does not make our relationship with God pure again. Paul declared in Philippians 3:13, "Brethren, I do not count myself to have apprehended; but one thing I do, forgetting those things which are behind and reaching forward to those things which are ahead."

King David sinned when he fell into adultery with Bathsheba and then, caught in a whirlwind of desperation, he had her husband killed in battle. The repercussions of these actions could have destroyed him, throwing him into the depths of despair and condemnation. David was at a crossroad in his life. Would he stifle the talent God had given him or would he repent and write a psalm? The answer is found so humbly put in Psalm 51. David made his way past harm, failure, and disappointment, and came to God with a broken spirit, a broken and contrite heart. In a state of sincere repentance, he asked God, the Creator of the universe, to create once again.

Create in me a clean heart, O God, and renew a steadfast spirit within me. Do not cast me away from Your presence, and do not take Your Holy Spirit from me. Restore to me the joy of Your salvation, and uphold me by Your generous Spirit. Psalm 51:10–12

David understood God's willingness to forgive and His ability to heal the past, to create anew and give a second chance. God is in the business of making clean hearts. We must believe in the power of mercy and the importance of going forward in newness of life. "There is therefore now no condemnation to those who are in Christ Jesus, who do not walk according to the flesh, but according to the Spirit" (Romans 8:1).

Sin, or feeling un-forgiven, stops creative flow in our lives. When David asked God to *create a clean heart*, he was not only asking God to restore communion, but also to make him useful again. Read what Psalm 51:13 says, "Then I will teach transgressors Your ways, and sinners shall be converted to You." After David's heart was made right before God, he began to let his light shine once more and witnessed to others about God's redeeming love.

Self-reproach hinders the birth of inspiration. It can add to insecurities that already grip our souls, especially if we feel condemnation from others. We may conclude that we don't have anything to offer people who are *more worthy* or *more righteous*. We not only keep ourselves from the blessing of creative actions, but others cannot benefit from our artistic expression, either. While caught in self-pity, there's no attempt to see the needs of others or to find innovative ways to encourage them through their own pain and disappointments. God can use our past to help others find their future. If you are stuck in the quicksand of remorse, it's time to pray, "Create in me a clean heart, O God, and renew a steadfast spirit within me."

If you have not repented of something—you should feel convicted and the need to repent as soon as possible. But if you have sincerely asked for God's forgiveness, then you're forgiven and your sin forgotten. God wants you to forget the past, live in the light of His word, and experience a more fruitful future.

Unfounded Guilt

Have you ever walked down a well-known path and found it feeling strangely unfamiliar? Maybe the sun was setting and you had never ventured that way at dusk. Perhaps a sudden storm caught you off guard, causing you to feel cold or anxious. Did strangers meet you unexpectedly and your out-going personality froze for fear of the unknown? We may relate to these or similar encounters, but they usually don't stop us from walking that way again.

Does the path of your life consist of specific boundaries? Most of us like to walk in the comfort of familiarity. We don't like it when things violate our space or disrupt our routine, but at least it's obvious when this happens. Yet when situations occur slowly over time, like twilight fading to darkness, our eyes adjust and we are unaware of just how dark it has become. This can really be disheartening.

A few years ago, I did some soul searching and as I thought about my life, I came to understand that others influenced me more than I had realized. Guilt became my worst enemy and a major hindrance to my artistic journey. Similar to dusk steadily creeping in, I didn't see this stumbling block until after I tripped. As you read on, think about your life. Have situations caught you off guard and caused you to lose your footing?

For starters, God has blessed me with a wonderful husband. I've been fortunate in that I could stay at home and raise our five beautiful children. Looking back at those early years, I realized every day brought new pleasures, such as teaching the children to read and then having the privilege of home schooling them. After school, I would take an hour or two and paint. I was healthy, happy, and very enthusiastic about life. I completed some of my best paintings during this season in my life. This pattern lasted for several years.

Slowly things changed. Comments got back to me, such as, "She is so lucky, she has everything." "She wouldn't be so happy if she were in my shoes." "It must be nice, not having to work." I began to feel guilty about the blessings of God. Consequently, I started painting less and doing more things around the house. I also made myself more available to help others when my children were older. As the years passed, close friends began saying things right to me, like, "You don't understand . . ." "You've never been through it, so how would you know?" This added to my guilt and I pushed myself even harder—no longer able to relax and enjoy life.

The result of my actions manifested in the form of fibromyalgia. I was officially miserable; the bounce had left my step and my strength was gone. In an effort to avoid the fatigue and pain, I pushed myself even harder. It didn't work though. The more I labored, the more the symptoms increased. Still, I felt guilty if I wasn't doing something for someone. Unfounded guilt is a powerful tool of the enemy. Even my service became unfruitful because I became frustrated and my conduct lacked grace. My creativity suffered as well, because I set it aside to do *more important* things or so my guilt-laden soul made me to believe.

With clear insight, I have since altered my course. I no longer feel badly for having the joy of the Lord or for the blessings He has bestowed. I also take time for myself again, time to paint, write, and quilt. At first, guilt tried to creep back into my heart, but through prayer, I was able to keep things in perspective. In addition, through the healing power of Jesus, my health has returned. The peace of God rules my heart, the joy of the Lord is my strength, and art is a part of my daily routine.

Alice, a widow in her 70's, told me, "I love to paint but often feel guilty because I think I should be busy doing other things; like going to the store for an elderly neighbor or visiting at the nursing home."

"We are called to serve," I admonished. "However, to feel guilty because you're participating in a creative outlet is not of God. Helping others is good and needful, but not at the expense of your own health and well-being, especially if it ends up hurting your witness."

"I know what you mean," Alice replied. "The times I don't experience guilt while painting, I feel refreshed, even energized." Her own words testify to the positive affects of creativity. Do you see how her creative outlet makes her stronger for the Lord's service? Like Alice, we all need to embrace the fact that we can do *both* our creative outlet, and labor for the Lord. The important thing is to focus on the one we're doing at the time, realizing they can also be one in the same. But if we constantly fret about what we could be doing, while working on art, we void the benefits of taking creative action.

Psalm 100:2 says, "Serve the LORD with gladness . . ." This verse is a good gauge to use when it comes to balancing our time. If all we ever do is for others, or for the Church, and we never take time to renew our strength, service becomes a drudge. Most of us will continue to serve because we know it's right; but if we're not careful, we will grow weary and resentful, destroying the very good we intend to accomplish.

Guilt is very destructive, especially when not founded in truth. God created us with the desire to create, so how could it be against His will to do so? If you feel badly about spending time on a creative outlet, you probably won't.

The story of Mary and Martha found in Luke10:38–42 makes a valid point.

> *Now it happened as they went that He (Jesus) entered a certain village; and a certain woman named Martha welcomed Him into her house. And she had a sister called Mary, who also sat at Jesus' feet and heard His word. But Martha was distracted with much serving, and she approached Him and said, 'Lord, do You not care that my sister has left me to serve alone? Therefore tell her to help me.' And Jesus answered and said to her, 'Martha, Martha, you are worried and troubled about many things. But one thing is needed, and Mary has chosen that good part, which will not be taken away from her.'*

We need to be servants and I'm sure Jesus and the others who were with Him that day were glad they ate . . . but truthfully; if serving is all we ever do and we don't spend time with Jesus, we will grow weary in well-doing. In Chapter Eight, we learned that writing, poetry, and song are all forms of creative worship and a way to draw near to God. I believe that using our creative outlets can actually be a way to spend time with Jesus. No matter what our outlets are, we can accomplish art and meditation simultaneously.

One word of caution, though, balance is important. We must not go to the other extreme and get so caught up in our creative outlets that we forget service—both are necessary. Moreover, there may be seasons when Jesus calls us to set aside some extra devotional time so He can refresh us and reveal His purpose. That way, when we return to the work of the Lord, we will be more effective. I will talk more about our God-given need for rest in the next chapter. However, to feel at fault simply for spending time on a creative outlet is wrong. In the long run, being creative will make us more productive for His service. When all we ever do is for others or busying ourselves with the cares of this life, like Martha, burn-out is inevitable. Even sickness can result and our ability to be useful to God diminishes. Do not allow any of these hindrances to artistic expression keep you from experiencing creative fulfillment or from completing God's will for your life.

chapter sixteen
the art of rest

And on the seventh day God ended His work which
He had done, and He rested on the seventh day from
all His work which He had done. Genesis 2:2

It took God six days to create our universe. "Then God saw everything that He had made, and indeed *it was* very good. So the evening
and the morning were the sixth day" (Genesis 1:31). Creation was
complete. Well, almost. The seventh day of creation came quietly and
without visible significance. What then makes this day important,
even necessary? Rest! God "rested from all His work which he had
done." Then He "blessed and sanctified it," and gave rest as a gift to
humanity (Genesis 2:3). Blessing and sanctification: we desire both in
our lives and yet so often they seem to elude us. In part, because we
do not take the need for relaxing seriously, nor do we understand the
inner workings of God's spirit to revitalize us through rest.

Performance and other issues push us onward. We yearn for

success in our finances, in position, and through accomplishments. But we've missed the point when a day of rest seems more like a punishment than a privilege. Jesus said, "The Sabbath was made for man, and not man for the Sabbath" (Mark 2:27). Yet in our culture, with its non-stop pace, the call to rest seems archaic—in spite of mental, emotional, and physical problems that affect so many because of this lifestyle.

Have you ever noticed how the Sabbath Day miracles had as much to do with healing heart attitudes as they did with healing the physical body? In each case, illnesses or deformities kept people from service, from using their talents for the Lord, and yet each person was healed while in a *place of rest*. To clarify, I'm not talking about a day of the week, but rather, a setting aside of time in which we can be refreshed.

As I go through a few of these Sabbath Day miracles, consider your own walk with the Lord. See if any of these examples could change your way of thinking about some situations you may be going through. In John 9, we find a man who was born blind and the first thing the disciples asked was, "Who sinned, this man or his parents, that he was born blind?" (vs. 2). Unfortunately, this mindset still exists today and people have a tendency to assume all defects are a result of sin or blame. Though this can be true because of addictions and diseases passed on to children at birth, it is not always the case! "Jesus answered, Neither this man nor his parents sinned, but that the works of God should be revealed in him" (vs. 3). When we don't understand God's ways, or His timing, we must still believe He has a purpose beyond what we can see or comprehend. Christianity truly is a walk of faith.

Jesus came to the blind man as the Potter, and anointed his eyes with fresh clay: the same substance used to make the first man, Adam. A miracle was about to take place, but first the blind man was told to go and wash. Why was this? I think it would be fair to say this man lived his entire life under the scrutiny of others and he suffered with insecurity and shame. Hence, the disciples' question, *who sinned...?*

His circumstances kept him from believing that God truly cared about him. Yet, while in a place of Sabbath rest, he came to understand that God had a goal and it wasn't his fault that he was born blind. Nevertheless, before his healing could take place, Jesus needed to change his way of thinking by requiring him to wash away the clay of a "woe is me" attitude. When he obeyed, he came again seeing, and glorified God! He went from sitting on a bench to becoming an active player in the plan of God.

Often, people who live with handicaps live with complexes and feel God could never use them. Then there are those who don't feel they are *good enough* for God because of personal flaws, even if they don't have a physical disability. They are spiritually blind, so to speak, and need a touch from God.

Another thing some of us fail to consider is God's timing. He has a destiny for each one of us, and what appears impossible or simply out of reach, can happen in a moment when Jesus chooses to show up.

In addition, we may not understand why some of our aspirations don't happen as quickly as we would like, especially if we *are* talented. However, God is more concerned about our integrity than our personal success. His eternal purpose is more important than our temporal feelings. Revelations 4:11 declares, "You are worthy, O Lord, to receive glory and honor and power; for You created all things, and by Your will they exist and were created." If you feel you haven't been given a fair chance to show and/or share your talents, or if opportunities seem to pass you by, seek the Lord. Inquire as to whether you may have some heart issues that need adjusting before doors can open. Once you do this, wait patiently for the Lord, for He is faithful to make a way, even if for now that way seems out of sight. Moreover, if you have fallen into a *woe is me* mindset, find a place of Sabbath rest. Spend time with Jesus and allow Him to anoint your eyes and show you what is required. "For it is God who works in you both to will and to do for His good pleasure" (Philippians 2:13). As we have learned throughout this book, there are personal benefits to being creative; yet ultimately God sees the bigger picture. He knows what He wants to accomplish, why He's given us the talents we have, and when He wants us to use them. In the meantime, God expects us to hone our skills and make ourselves available, so that when the call comes, we will be ready.

Luke 13 tells of a woman with a spirit of infirmity. She was so weak she could not straighten herself. Bowed by circumstance, all she could see were the things of the earth. Her perspective kept her from seeing things through the eyes of God. How we look at our circumstances or even ourselves will affect our thoughts, our talents, and ultimately our labors, either for good or for bad. The inability to function, or *burnout* in modern terms, results when we can't let go of things, even while away from them. For example, we may bring stress home from work, which doesn't allow for a needed break. We may be worn down from the prolonged care and concern for others, such as a sick or elderly family member, a child or spouse who is in the military and stationed overseas. Other stressors include financial difficulties, opinionated in-laws, or relationships gone bad, be it a spouse, a child, or a dear friend. When there is no mental or emotional rest, these things all lead to exhaustion. Busy lifestyles also have a tendency to change our point of view and can cause us to take our eyes off "the prize of the upward call of God in Christ Jesus" (Philippians 3:14). God designed us with the need to rest: spirit, soul, and body—when ignored, burnout is inevitable.

The Psalmist declared, "I will lift up my eyes to the hills—From whence comes my help" (Psalm 121:1). He knew he couldn't overcome adversity in his own strength or by focusing on the things around him. The woman with the spirit of infirmity learned this while in a place of Sabbath rest. Along with receiving physical strength, she saw the world differently, and she glorified God.

Luke 6 speaks of another Sabbath day miracle: the man with a withered hand. This defect represents the inability to labor to our full potential. We may not have a withered hand in the natural, but constant labor without rest can cause us to shrivel up in our attitudes and become withdrawn. One major hindrance to creative flow is the need to impress. Even participating in helpful services can keep us busier than God requires at times. For example, after a long days work we engage in church activities, community service, committee meetings, or revolve our lives around the children: having play dates, taking them to sporting events, dance classes, or music lessons, at the risk of losing ourselves. Yes, these things are needed and worthy of recognition. But when our emotional circulation is *cut off* for lack of rejuvenation, a withered hand attitude becomes a factor and no one remembers our good works. They just wonder why we're so moody or why we're not as active as we once were, though neither are a fair assessment.

The impotent man lying by the pool of Bethesda, found in John 5, was so feeble that he could not help himself, nor did anyone else try to assist him. One purpose for this Sabbath day miracle is to show us we cannot rely on our own ability or the arm of flesh to receive strength. But then many of us are on the other side of this story. We are strong and feel invincible; convinced we don't need to slow down or occasionally stop. Yet Isaiah 40:30 warns, "Even the youths shall faint and be weary, and the young men shall utterly fall." God is not impressed with our natural strength. "But those who wait on the LORD shall renew their strength; they shall mount up with wings like eagles, they shall run and not be weary, they shall walk and not faint" (Isaiah 40:31).

Waiting on the Lord not only strengthens our spirit, it increases our energy levels, both emotionally and physically, so we can better cope with life and more efficiently fulfill our purpose here on earth. I realize there may be occasions where God brings supernatural strength to sustain us for longer than normal. For example, we may help during the aftermath of a natural disaster. Though it's grueling and time consuming, God will bless our efforts because they are needful. Even this should be temporary, though. We must recognize when God's grace lifts and He calls us back to a place of rest and waiting upon the Lord. Here our strength can return and make us ready for more labor.

When it comes to getting things done, it's easy to believe the more time we invest the more we can achieve, which leaves no room for legitimate rest. In reality, the more we obey God's word and follow the leading of His Spirit, the more we will accomplish—even when His direction includes a time of stillness and prayer. "Wait on the LORD; be of good courage, and He shall strengthen your heart; wait, I say, on the LORD!" (Psalm 27:14).

We must approach quiet times with an attitude of peace. Fretting and feeling guilty if we're not busy eliminates any opportunity for rejuvenation. Ambition is great and action is necessary, but these things can become idols to us. Hebrews 12:1 says, " . . . let us lay aside every weight, and the sin which so easily ensnares us, and let us run with endurance the race that is set before us." God is calling us to lay aside some weights, distractions so to speak, that we might better run this race at His pace and not our own.

God is faithful to bring seasons of repose, but we must take advantage of them when they come. No doubt, the most important thing we can do with our time and talents is use them for God. Nevertheless, there may be occasions when our zeal for witnessing wanes or our service for the Lord becomes wearisome. If not careful, we could lose sight of God's purpose and harden our hearts toward His voice and His will. This leads to a greater problem: it limits our ability to receive fresh insight and strength. Over the years, I've known people who fell away from the Lord because they did not find that secret place where God could renew their strength and keep their heart attitudes pure. Psalm 62:5 admonishes, "My soul, wait silently for God alone, for my expectation is from Him." Waiting on the Lord guarantees strength, which improves our ability to do the work of the Lord successfully.

Seasons

God designed the seasons to provide regular intervals of sowing, growing, harvest, and rest. We can't change, speed up, or even slow down any of these seasons. Then He went a step further and instructed His people to give the land rest every seventh year. This rest revitalized the soil, which sustained its ability to produce at maximum levels and preserved mineral content. God provided food in the seventh year when His people obeyed His voice, but He did not prosper their efforts when they ignored His command and planted (Leviticus 25:2–7). Now, apply this principle on a personal level. If we do not sow our talents, we cannot reap. However, if we never relax, it will deplete our ability to bring forth a healthy harvest. In Matthew 11:28–30 Jesus calls us to,

> *"Come to Me, all you who labor and are heavy laden, and I will give you rest. Take My yoke upon you and learn from Me, for I am gentle and lowly in heart, and you will find rest for your souls. For My yoke is easy and My burden is light."*

The word *rest* in this verse means *intermission*, which does not necessarily mean an extended break, but rather a pause to regroup. There will always be more for us to do on the other side of every break, but keep in mind, the respite must be long enough to make a difference. When the yoke of labor becomes heavy, even in our creative endeavors, we should stop and consider if we're doing too much. There will be times when fresh ideas tarry, and yet forcing the issue could mean walking outside of God's present provision. Our creative output will diminish if we never give it rest. God expects productivity and increase from our lives, but He also knows when it's time to stop.

Prayer and meditation embody the art of rest by bringing inner peace. They also make us more receptive to supernatural direction. While in a constant state of activity, even when it's for God's service, we can over-extend ourselves and become easily agitated. We should never put *good works* above our personal relationship with Jesus, which is His ultimate goal. Spending time at the Lord's feet will verify our purpose, so we know when it's time to labor and when it's time to hold back—when its time to be as Mary, or time to act as Martha (Luke10:38–42). This doesn't make sense to the natural mind, but if God is calling us to rest and we don't heed His bidding, our labors will be in vain. Better to move forward at His pace, knowing His presence will carry us to success when the timing is right.

Jesus admonished in Matthew 11:29, " . . . and learn from me. . ." Part of that learning is to accept rest as a crucial element for continued strength and creative inspiration. Labor follows every season of repose, just as spring follows winter with the need to plant, followed by summer tending, and a fall harvest. Even as God controls natural seasons, so He determines the duration of our activities, including rest, but if we disregard His preeminence, we are asking for trouble. We can only be as good for service as we are strong in our walk with God and obedient to His will.

Creativity and Rest

If the Almighty God rested from His creative endeavors, we should follow His example, especially considering the limitations of our human strength and abilities. A time to replenish emotionally as well as physically, brings us to a place where fresh ideas can break forth, worthy of our time and effort. Even laboring on the same project for weeks at a time can become a bit overwhelming. Setting it aside for a day or two (longer if needed) renews creative vision. We can even take this concept and simplify it. While working on a piece of art, try looking away every now and then, for at least 30 seconds, this keeps everything from blurring all together. Appropriate intervals of rest improve artistic outcome!

Creative outlets require respites just like physical and emotional exertion. Many of us could choose to overlook the warning signals and still be able to create through sheer ability. If the push continues, though, inspiration and diversity will wear thin, causing less than favorable results. In comparison, if we stress our physical bodies and don't allow for adequate rest, fatigue takes hold, physical problems ensue, and the zest for life fades. The same thing happens emotionally and spiritually when we're not careful.

Blocked Creatives

"Blocked creatives" is a term the art world uses when creative ideas stop coming or excuses get in the way of creative activity. Most artists—no matter what their outlet—have felt blocked at one time or another. Fortunately, there are things we can do to help us get back on track. But before seeking motivation from books, galleries, concerts, and other such things, pray and ask God if He has allowed this dry spell for a reason. Is He calling you to draw near to Him, requiring stillness and meditation over action? Have you ever gotten so busy that weeks went by before you realized your quiet times had become few and far between? I have, and what caught my attention was the fact that my moods began to dictate my responses.

Creativity can strengthen us emotionally. It brings growth to our personality and enhances our ability to minister to others. However, this does not protect us from abusing its effectiveness by over doing. Adding pressure to our creative outlets by straining for new ideas or setting unreasonable deadlines can cause a different kind of block— our capacity to receive inspiration from God. This does not mean art requires a spiritual premise; but it should be done with a purpose in mind, even if that purpose is simply to relax. When we are open to the leading of God's Spirit, we will be more apt to produce things that go beyond us to a world that must have something to remind them of their need for God.

I'm the kind of person who likes being busy and getting things done, to the point of excess; yet I've learned to appreciate seasons of rest. Ecclesiastes 3:1 helped change my way of thinking. It says, "To everything there is a season, a time for every purpose under heaven." The next eight verses put life into perspective, making it easier to accept the seasons God has prepared for each one of us. He has a purpose and if that purpose is rest, then we best take advantage of it; knowing this too shall come to an end and labor will begin anew.

A while back, my computer crashed and it was a few weeks before I could get it fixed. I admit I was a little tense for the first two days because I couldn't work on my book, but then it hit me, "Arleen, God is calling you to give it a rest!" Peace came when I acknowledged the time off as a good thing. After I finally got my computer back, things seemed to flow more smoothly and I was thankful for the break.

Creativity follows the same principle as exercise. Bodily exercise boosts our endurance and increases the movement of endorphins causing us to feel better, but when over done, we can become addicted to our own adrenaline. Add that to an unwillingness to ever slow down and it causes a wearing out of our immune system. What once contributed to health and wholeness, even bringing about physical and emotional highs, now causes pain, fatigue, and frustration. We must give our bodies ample rest if we want to stay strong. This holds true with anything we allow to take large amounts of our time and energy, if it doesn't include some time to relax.

Finding Rest Through Creative Action

Creative outlets can serve as an escape from the daily grind, becoming a time of rest for us—no pressure, just pleasure from doing art. It's good to have at least one creative channel simply for fun, especially if your other talents are used for service, monetary purposes, or if they come with deadlines. The balance is in knowing when art refreshes and when it becomes another form of work.

Fatigue not only affects our bodies; passion dissipates, peace becomes elusive, simple tasks seem overwhelming, and the light of God grows dim. When these warning signals emerge, we must heed the call to rest. I learned this the hard way. There came a point in my life where I continually put others and their needs before mine, at the expense of my own health and well-being. I fell into the pattern of *good works* and felt guilty if I did anything for me. Even after the grip of exhaustion tightened, I still kept busy, pushing myself past physical and emotional limits, doing more than God required. Then the grave reality hit me that if I didn't choose to change my lifestyle, destruction would inevitably follow. I found that writing, painting, or quilting, along with taking personal time, actually empowered me and renewed my ability to assist others.

I'm sure many of you have laid down your lives for others and that's an admirable part of Christian living, but it shouldn't come to the point of destroying your health, your happiness, or most importantly, your witness for Jesus. When we begin to lose our ability to serve the Lord with gladness, we need to step back and pray for guidance. I firmly believe that if we will allow ourselves times of refreshing and occasionally walk away from the front lines of service, in the long run we will serve the Lord, and others, more effectively! God ordained it to be so and He has a purpose for every situation and season in our lives. No detail has been overlooked and His provision includes stillness and contemplation.

A friend of mine told me once, that quite often, while working on art, it becomes a time of worship for her. As she draws or paints, she can feel the presence of God, which moves her thoughts toward His goodness and she is refreshed. Do you find your creative outlet refreshing? Does it help you to keep things in perspective? Being creative is a part of our inherent nature, something God intended for our good. The blessings that come from taking time to create will affect more than the finished product. The strength we gain and the vitality we feel will carry into our daily routines, improve our attitudes, and bless those we interact with on a regular basis.

Our outlook on life and the pace at which we live has a lot to do with the art of rest. It will also determine our willingness to pursue creative outlets and how effective they can become—both personally and on a larger scale.

One Final Thought

As I bring this book to a close, don't only think about how to increase your creative abilities, pray, and ask Jesus to show you how to find your purpose. Evaluate the process by which you live your life. Decide if what fills the in-betweens, the every day stuff, is worth the stress you live with to succeed. Is the pressure something you can minimize by weighing your goals against an eternal standard? When we value temporal things, on an eternal scale, it throws everything out of balance. It distorts our view of what's important and ensnares us so that we cannot fully appreciate the life God has given us. "You will show me the path of life; in Your presence is fullness of joy; at Your right hand are pleasures forevermore" (Psalm16:11).

When we stay close to the Lord, He will direct our paths and reveal His good pleasure to us. It is our duty to use our talents; it is His responsibility to bring increase. May we work together to advance the Kingdom of our Lord Jesus Christ here on earth and trust that someday we shall hear, "Well done, good and faithful servant; you were faithful over a few things, I will make you ruler over many things. Enter into the joy of your Lord" (Matthew 25:21).

Selah ~ Stop and think about it.

appendix
plan of salvation

When God made man, he was without sin and created to live forever. Then Genesis 2:15–17 tells us,

> *Then the LORD God took the man and put him in the garden of Eden to tend and keep it. And the LORD God commanded the man, saying, of every tree of the garden you may freely eat; but of the tree of the knowledge of good and evil you shall not eat, for in the day that you eat of it you shall surely die.*

Chapter 3 of Genesis tells us that Adam and Eve disobeyed God and partook of that which was forbidden. The punishment? Death! And that punishment has been passed on to all of humanity through the tainted blood of Adam. Romans 3:23 says, "For all have sinned and fall short of the glory of God." Romans 6:23 goes on to say, "For the wages of sin is death, but the gift of God is eternal life in Christ Jesus our Lord." 1 Corinthians 15:22 concludes, "For as in Adam all die, even so in Christ all shall be made alive."

We had no choice; we were all born in sin and the punishment of that sin is death. Death, on the other hand, had no power over Jesus because He never sinned, and that is why He was able to rise from the dead. Jesus' blood is pure because He was born of a virgin and His Father is God. This is what makes His sacrifice acceptable to God and His provision for our sins to be forgiven. Romans 5:6–8 tells us,

> *For when we were still without strength, in due time Christ died for the ungodly. For scarcely for a righteous man will one*

die; yet perhaps for a good man someone would even dare to die. But God demonstrates His own love toward us, in that while we were still sinners, Christ died for us.

First, we must REPENT of our sins. 1 John 1:8–9 tell us, "If we say that we have no sin, we deceive ourselves, and the truth is not in us. If we confess our sins, He is faithful and just to forgive us our sins and to cleanse us from all unrighteousness."

Next, we must ACCEPT Jesus into our lives. John 1:12 says, "But as many as received Him, to them He gave the right to become children of God, to those who believe in His name." Ephesians 2:8–9 tells us, "For by grace you have been saved through faith, and that not of yourselves; it is the gift of God, not of works, lest anyone should boast." Then we must CONFESS that we believe. Romans 10:9–10 declares,

That if you confess with your mouth the Lord Jesus and believe in your heart that God has raised Him from the dead, you will be saved. For with the heart one believes unto righteousness, and with the mouth confession is made unto salvation.

If you do not know Jesus personally and have not accepted Him into your life, you can do it today. All you have to do is pray ~ acknowledge your need for the savior and *repent* of your sins. By faith, (believing in your heart) *accept* the fact that Jesus' death on the cross paid your spiritual debt so that your sins are now forgiven. Ask Jesus to come into your heart and make His abode there. Then *confess* (make it known to others) that Jesus Christ is your personal Lord and Savior. Rejoice! You now have eternal life through Him. May the Lord Jesus bless you abundantly as you begin your new life with new hope and new purpose. Amen.

author contact information

If you would like to contact the author,
you can email Arleen Jennings at:

arleen.jennings@gmail.com

TATE PUBLISHING & *Enterprises*

Tate Publishing is commited to excellence in the publishing industry.
Our staff of highly trained professionals, including editors, graphic
designers, and marketing personnel, work together to produce the
very finest books available. The company reflects the philosophy
established by the founders, based on Psalms 68:11,

"THE LORD GAVE THE WORD AND GREAT WAS THE COMPANY
OF THOSE WHO PUBLISHED IT."

If you would like further information, please call
1.888.361.9473
or visit our website
www.tatepublishing.com

TATE PUBLISHING & *Enterprises*, LLC
127 E. Trade Center Terrace
Mustang, Oklahoma 73064 USA